MATERIALS

PETER D. RILEY

First published in Great Britain by Heinemann Library
Halley Court, Jordan Hill, Oxford OX2 8EJ
a division of Reed Educational and Professional Publishing Ltd.
Heinemann is a registered trademark of Reed Educational & Professional Publishing Limited.

OXFORD FLORENCE PRAGUE MADRID ATHENS
MELBOURNE AUCKLAND KUALA LUMPUR SINGAPORE TOKYO
IBADAN NAIROBI KAMPALA JOHANNESBURG GABORONE
PORTSMOUTH NH CHICAGO MEXICO CITY SAO PAULO

Designed by Visual Image
Printed in Hong Kong

02 01 00 99 98
10 9 8 7 6 5 4 3 2 1

ISBN 0 431 08434 3

British Library Cataloguing in Publication Data

Riley, Peter, 1947-
Materials - (Cycles in science)
1.Materials - Juvenile literature 2.Recycling (Waste, etc.) - Juvenile literature 3.Metamorphosis - Juvenile literature
I.Title
363.7'282

Acknowledgements

The Publishers would like to thank the following for permission to reproduce photographs:
Bubbles: R Livermore p8; Bruce Coleman Ltd: A Davies p26, C Lockwood p12, H Reinhard p21; Michael Holford: p28; Planet Earth Pictures: B Brown p15, A Jones p11, P Scoones p10; Science Photo Library: D Guyon p20, R Maisonneuve p14, NASA p29, D Parker p7, S Stammers p17; Tony Stone: (Images) P Chesley p9, P Harris p16, R Magnusson p6, J Willis p18, (Worldwide) S Jauncey p13, M Leman p22; Trip: H Rogers p24; ZEFA: pp 4, 19, Faltner p23, RGN p25, Ricatto p27, Rossenbach p5.

Cover photograph reproduced with permission of Dr Jeremy Burgess, Science Photo Library

Our thanks to Jim Drake for his comments in the preparation of this book.

Every effort has been made to contact copyright holders of any material reproduced in this book. Any omissions will be rectified in subsequent printings if notice is given to the Publisher.

Any words appearing in the text in bold, **like this**, are explained in the Glossary.

CONTENTS

MATERIALS

Can you guess what is made of wood fibres, clay or chalk, wax and ***pigments****? You are looking at it. It is this page. The wood fibres make up most of the paper. Particles of clay, or chalk, stick to the fibres and make the paper stronger and more* ***opaque****. The wax makes the paper more water-resistant and helps the ink stick to the paper. The pigments, which make the colours of the ink, come from oil. The oil is made from the bodies of ancient sea creatures that lived millions of years ago. Each one of the substances wood, clay, chalk, wax or pigment is a* ***material****. If this sheet of paper contains so many different materials from different places, imagine how many materials make up a car!*

PROPERTIES OF MATERIALS

A material has a range of useful **properties**. It may be hard and strong like steel or it may be soft and flexible. Many of the things we use, like this book, are made from more than one material. Each material is important because it has at least one useful property that the others do not. For example, the wood fibres in this page are not water resistant so they are coated with wax to prevent them falling apart if they get wet.

Cotton is a renewable material.

Rock is a non-renewable material.

NATURAL AND MANUFACTURED

We use thousands of different materials. Some materials, like the wood fibres and the clay particles in this paper, are formed from natural materials. Other materials, like the pigments making these letters, are made by a series of processes which change one material into another. Materials which are changed greatly to make new materials are called raw materials. Oil, for example, is the raw material used for making pigments. The processes in which a raw material is used to make a new material are called the manufacturing processes and the new material is called a manufactured material.

RENEWABLE AND NON-RENEWABLE

We never run out of some materials. They are produced by plants and animals every year. Two examples of these renewable materials are cotton and wool. Most materials are non-renewable. When they have been used up there is no more to replace them. Oil and metal ores are examples of non-renewable materials. As the human population grows, more and more materials are needed. We can save, or conserve, the stock of non-renewable materials on the planet by recycling materials we have already used.

WHAT ARE MATERIALS MADE FROM?

From early times people have wondered about materials and their properties. They formed ideas about them but most of these ideas were later shown to be wrong. One idea, about the elements, is still used today and has helped scientists understand the structure and the properties of materials. This information is still being used in developing new materials and recycling old ones.

ARE YOU MADE OF FIRE?

The first person in history to think about what things were made of was an ancient Greek **philosopher** called Thales. He believed that everything was made from the same basic substance, or element. He thought that as living things need water for life, then everything must be made of different forms of water. Other ancient Greek philosophers did not agree. Eventually it was decided that everything must be made from a mixture of four elements – water, air, fire and earth. This idea was used by scientists for more than 2000 years. You may still hear people today talk about the wind and rain as 'the elements'.

Many years ago, fire, water, air and earth were considered the four basic elements from which everything was made.

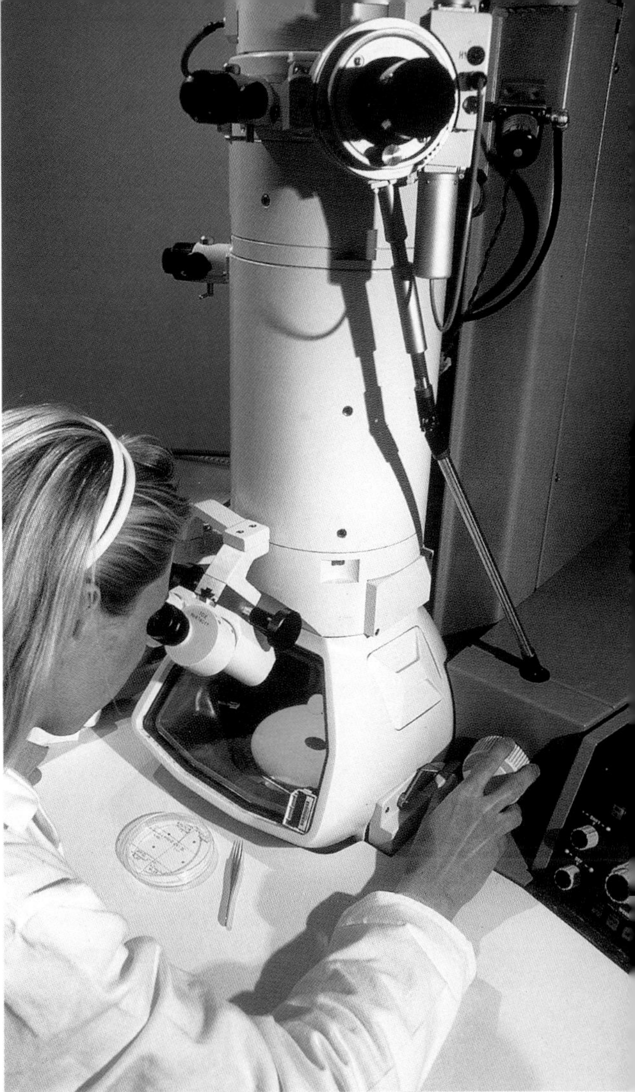

WHAT ARE THINGS REALLY MADE OF?

In 1661 an English scientist called Robert Boyle began testing the ancient Greeks' idea that materials were made from four elements. He discovered that air, water and earth could be broken down into simpler substances. We call these substances elements. For example, water is made from two elements called hydrogen and oxygen. So far, 109 elements have been discovered.

HOW SMALL CAN YOU GET?

What would happen if you took something and cut it in two, then took one half and cut that in two and so on? Eventually you would get to something so small that it could not be divided up any more. A Greek philosopher called Democritus had this idea over 2000 years ago. He called the smallest **particle** an atom, which is Greek for 'indivisible'. We still use his idea today although particles smaller than atoms have been discovered.

This **electron microscope** is being used to investigate the structure of materials. Some electron microscopes are so powerful that the arrangement of atoms within a material can be clearly seen.

ELEMENTS, ATOMS AND RECYCLING

Scientists use their knowledge of how materials are made from elements, and how the atoms of elements join together, when they make new materials. They also use this knowledge to find new ways of recycling materials.

THE STATES OF MATTER

Materials can exist in three ways. These are the three forms, or states, of matter. Materials change from one state to another when they reach a certain temperature. These temperature changes occur naturally. They can also be made to happen. Heat is used in manufacturing new materials or recycling old ones, so materials may change states during these processes too.

THREE STATES OF MATTER

Gas, liquid and solid are the three states of matter. The air is a mixture of gases and water is the most common liquid on this planet. Hailstones, which bounce off your head in a hailstorm, are solid while their temperature is low. But, when they warm up they melt into a liquid and then **evaporate** into a gas.

Carbon dioxide gas is squashed into drinks in cans and bottles.

What is your state of matter? Think of your bones, blood and lungs.

HOW CAN YOU TELL THEM APART?

A solid has a definite shape and **volume**. A liquid has no definite shape but it has a definite volume and it can be poured. A gas has no definite shape or volume. Unlike solids and liquids you can squash a gas and make it fill a smaller space. When you release it from a container, such as an aerosol spray can, it will spread out and fill any available space.

ALL CHANGE

All materials have melting points and boiling points. The melting point is the temperature at which a solid turns into a liquid. The boiling point is the temperature at which a liquid turns into a gas. Each substance has melting and boiling points that are different from other substances. The melting point of ice is 0 °C and the boiling point of water is 100 °C.

CHANGING STATES IN THE MATERIAL CYCLE

When iron ore is heated strongly with coke (made from coal) and limestone, the metal iron is released from the rock. This change takes place at such a high temperature that the metal is **molten**. It is poured into huge heat-resistant buckets to be taken away from the **furnace** to cool down and become solid again.

Glass that is collected from a recycling centre is mixed with raw materials for making new glass. The mixture is heated strongly so the raw materials can form new molten glass and the recycled glass also melts and mixes with it.

The molten rock flowing down the side of the **volcano** will cool and turn into a solid again.

THE WATER CYCLE

Water is changed by four processes. They take place at normal temperatures on the Earth and allow water to exist in three forms on this planet. The processes are also a part of the water cycle which is the largest and fastest material cycle on the planet.

THE CHANGING STATES OF WATER

Ice is solid water. When ice melts it becomes liquid water. Liquid water turns back into solid water by freezing at 0 °C. These processes are easy to see. The changes from liquid water to water **vapour** and back again are more difficult to observe.

Water changes from liquid into vapour by **evaporation**. In this process tiny **particles** of water escape from the liquid surface. Water vapour is a gas and mixes with the other gases in the air. Evaporation takes place faster in warmer conditions than in colder conditions.

The ice in this **glacier** is breaking up and toppling into the water. Eventually, the ice will melt into water, the next stage in the water cycle.

Tiny particles of water escape from the lake's surface into the air. They form a vapour that usually cannot be seen. But in the cool air above this lake they have condensed to form tiny droplets which can be seen as a mist.

Water vapour changes back into liquid water by **condensation**. Droplets of water form on cool dust particles in the air and make a mist or cloud. They also form on cool surfaces. Your breath contains water vapour and when you breathe out onto a window pane the vapour condenses onto the cold glass.

ROUND AND ROUND

A large amount of water evaporates from the surfaces of oceans, seas and lakes every day. It forms water vapour that rises into the air until it cools, condenses and forms water droplets that make clouds. When clouds reach cold regions over land they release their water as rain. This happens because the water droplets in the cloud freeze and form snowflakes. The snowflakes are too heavy to stay in the air so they fall through the clouds. As they fall they reach warmer air and melt, then they fall to the ground as drops of water. The rainwater forms streams and rivers which flow back to the oceans, seas and lakes where the water cycle can begin again.

WATER AND YOU

Water is the main material in our bodies. Wherever people live there is a demand for clean water. Water is also used in food production and making other materials. Water is needed all the time so ways are being found to provide a constant supply from the water cycle.

WATER AND YOU

You are awash with water. Nearly three-quarters of your weight is due to the amount of water in your body. You are thinking about this with a brain that is nearly four-fifths water and holding this book with bones that are much drier – less than a third of their weight is due to the water in them.

CLEANING UP WATER

Water rushing down a river carries twigs, grit, clay and **micro-organisms**. Before it can gush out of your tap, the water must be cleaned. First, the water passes through a metal grill which removes large objects like twigs and plastic bags.

These sprays are carefully positioned so the water reaches all the newly planted crops.

Second, chemicals called alum and lime are added. These stick to any clay and silt floating in the water and make them sink. Third, the water passes through a filter made of sand and gravel to trap any remaining **particles** in the water. Fourth, chlorine or ozone is bubbled through the water to kill the micro-organisms. Look at your next drink of water and think about what it has been through.

Waste water from a town goes to a sewage works where it is cleaned and released into a river.

USE OF WATER

Water is needed for growing crops and raising farm animals. Huge amounts of water are used to make all the different things around us. For example, it takes 8 litres of water to make a litre of lemonade and 30,000 litres of water to make all the items in a car – from its steel body to its rubber tyres.

SUPPLYING DEMAND

The amount of water in a river varies through the year as the weather changes between dry and wet weather. A river cannot supply a constant amount of water so a **dam** might be built across it to flood a valley and make a reservoir. Some places do not receive enough rainfall. Water is transported to these places along underground pipes from distant reservoirs.

This dam has trapped the river water behind it to fill the valley and give a constant supply of water.

LIVING THINGS

Plants and animals provide us with renewable materials. The materials they make as they grow are essential in their lives but humans can make use of these materials too.

THE CYCLE OF LIFE

Plants make food using the energy from sunlight, carbon dioxide from the air and water and **minerals** from the soil. They use the food to grow and to reproduce. Animals eat the plants and use the food for growth and reproduction too. When plants and animals die their bodies rot away and form carbon dioxide in the air and minerals in the soil. They are recycled with water and more sunlight into more living things. The materials we use from living things such as wood, **fibres** and leather are renewable as they are part of the life cycle of plants or animals.

This material, which looks like snow, is wood **pulp** that is about to be flattened into sheets of paper. A sample is being taken to check the wood pulp process is working correctly.

WOOD

Wood is a strong material made by trees to hold up leaves to the sunlight. It is made from tiny pipes and fibres which are arranged in rings inside the trunk and branches. The shape and thickness of the fibres give the wood its **properties**. The wood may be light in weight and easily cut like the balsa wood used in model aeroplanes or it may be hard and tough like the wood in a ball used in a game of bowls.

Paper is made by separating the fibres in the wood and making them into a pulp.

These sheep are being shorn. Their thick, woolly coats will be used to make wool for clothing.

COTTON

Cotton plants make seeds covered in fibres (see picture on page 4). The fibres are removed and twisted into threads called cotton yarn. This is woven into cotton shirts, denim jeans and other clothes.

WOOL

Wool is made from fibres which grow out of a sheep's skin. The wavy fibres are covered in scales and under the microscope look a little like crocodile tails. The wavy, scaly structure of the fibres stops them packing too closely together and allows air to get trapped between them. The air stops heat quickly passing out of the sheep's body and keeps it warm. This makes wool a good heat insulator and woollen yarn is used in clothes to keep you warm.

LEATHER

Leather is made from the skins of cattle which are called hides. Inside the skin is a network of fibres which make the skin strong and flexible. After processing the hide, the fibres still remain to make a strong flexible material for shoes and boots.

ROCKS

The cycle of rocks through the environment is very slow. Rocks may come from below the Earth's surface or they may form on the surface or in the sea. Rocks are made from crystals of minerals which may change if the rocks are heated.

The pebbles in this stream bed have come from the rocks in the mountains beyond the bridge.

THE ROCK CYCLE

The Earth has a rocky **crust**. Underneath is a hot, semi-liquid rocky interior. The heat melts the rock in the lower part of the crust. The **molten** rock moves upwards. It may become trapped in the crust and cool down slowly to form **granite** or it may escape through the mouth of a **volcano** and cool down quickly to form **basalt**. Rocks which form in this way are called igneous rocks (see picture on page 9).

Rock is affected by the weather. When water gets into cracks and freezes, the ice that forms pushes the rock apart and breaks it into pieces. These are carried by rivers. The smallest **particles** eventually settle down and form a layer of sand. In time, the layer gets so thick and heavy that the particles are squashed together and form **sandstone**. These rocks are called sedimentary rocks.

The Earth's crust is divided into huge slabs called **plates**. The movement of the semi-liquid rock beneath them pushes some of them together. Where this happens one plate is forced under the other. The rocks in the sinking plate get hot and the cycle can begin again. The rock cycle takes hundreds of millions of years.

ROCKS FROM SHELLS

Many sea creatures make shells for protection. They use chemicals dissolved in the sea water to make their shells. When the creatures die their shells sink to the sea bed and form a layer. In time, as more die, the layer gets thicker and heavier and turns into rock. Limestone and chalk are both formed in this way.

ROCKS AND MINERALS

Rocks are made from crystals that interlock and make them strong. The crystals are made from minerals. A mineral is a substance that is made from one or more elements. For example, a common mineral found in many kinds of rock is silica. It is made from the elements called silicon and oxygen.

CHANGING FORMS

Some of the rocks in the Earth's crust are squashed together as the plates move. They form new mountain ranges. The pressure, due to squashing, heats the rocks strongly over a long time. The rock crystals melt and reform in a different way. The changed rock is called metamorphic rock.

The fossil of the hard body of this ancient sea creature can be seen on the surface of this piece of limestone.

ROCKY MATERIALS

Rocks have properties that make them particularly useful for building. Clay is formed from rocks and is used in building and making pottery. Limestone is used in making cement and forms part of a mixture with sand to make glass – a rocky material that humans can help recycle.

USING ROCKS

Igneous rocks like **granite** and **basalt** are very hard and are used for making concrete. The **mineral crystals** in granite are large and make the rock look attractive when its surface is polished. Polished granite blocks are used as decoration for the front of important buildings like museums and banks. They form part of the supporting structure too.

Sedimentary rocks form thick hard layers or beds. Between the layers are boundaries called bedding planes where the rocks are easier to cut. **Sandstone** and limestone are used as building stone because they are strong but easy to cut into small sizes.

Marble and slate are metamorphic rocks. Marble is a strong rock with an attractive surface and is used for decoration. Slate splits into thin waterproof sheets and is used as a roofing material.

When clay is mixed with water it is easy to mould and shape.

CLAY

Clay is made from very small **particles** that form when rocks like granite are **weathered**. Different types of clay are used for making bricks and pottery.

The clay is mixed with water and shaped into a brick or a cup. Then it is heated strongly in a **furnace** called a kiln. The heat makes the tiny particles stick together where they touch and form a rigid structure which is strong but brittle.

CEMENT AND CONCRETE

Cement is made by heating limestone and clay together. It is used to join bricks in a wall or gravel in concrete. When water is added to cement it forms interlocking crystals that bind bricks together or make concrete set hard.

GLASS

Sand, limestone and a chemical called soda are heated together to make glass. Glass is a hard, strong, transparent substance which cleans easily and does not rot. Sheets of glass are used in windows because they let in light but keep out wind and rain without weathering like rock.

RECYCLING ROCKY MATERIALS

When old stone buildings are pulled down, the stones may be used to build something else or they may be crushed and used in the foundations of roads. Clay cannot be recycled but glass can. Recycling glass saves sand, limestone and soda. Less energy is used to recycle glass than to make it from raw **materials**, so fuels are saved too.

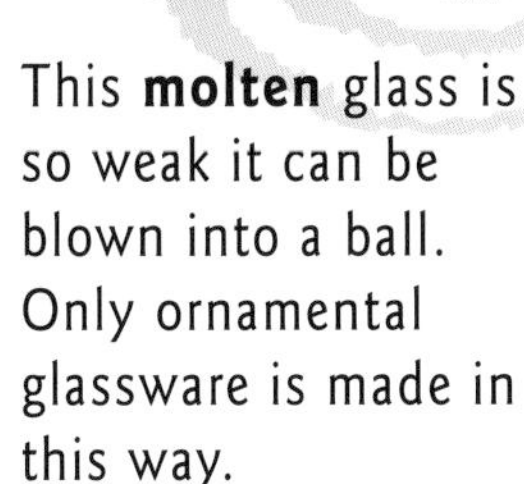

This **molten** glass is so weak it can be blown into a ball. Only ornamental glassware is made in this way.

METALS

Metals have many useful properties and are used to make a wide range of things. Very few metals are found in their pure metallic state. Most metals are found in rocks called ores. Energy is needed to release the metal from the ore once it has been mined. Large amounts of iron and aluminium are recycled.

Red hot steel from a **furnace** is being rolled into a thin sheet.

PROPERTIES AND USES OF METALS

Metals are strong shiny **materials** that can be shaped or pulled into long thin wires. They are good **conductors** of electricity and heat. These properties have been used in a variety of ways to make a huge range of items. Cars and lorries, wristwatches, cutlery, pans, zips, coins and the wire in a light bulb are all made of metals.

THE AGES OF METAL

Most metals are naturally combined with other substances in rocks called ores. Nearly 4000 years ago, tin was discovered by heating rocks. It was mixed with copper, which is found naturally, to make a stronger metal called bronze. The period of time when most metal objects were made of bronze is called the Bronze Age.

About 2500 years ago people learnt how to increase the heat in a fire with **bellows** and discovered that certain rocks would release iron. Iron is stronger than bronze so metal workers changed over to using it. This was the beginning of the Iron Age. Iron is still the main metal we use today. Much of it is changed into steel.

ALUMINIUM – THE LATE ARRIVAL

Aluminium is the most common metal on the Earth but huge amounts of energy are needed to release it from its ore. In 1886 two chemists, Charles Hall and Paul Heroult, discovered a way of extracting aluminium easily by using electricity. Today the strong, lightweight properties of aluminium are used to make bodies for aircraft and coaches, and the cables for overhead power lines. Aluminium is not poisonous and does not contaminate food, so it is used to make drink cans and thin sheets of it are used for wrapping all kinds of food to keep them fresh.

RECYCLING METALS

Up to half of the iron and aluminium in use today will be recycled. This will save some of the non-renewable ores and fuel and energy needed to **extract** the metals.

The steel in these old car bodies will be taken back to the steelworks and mixed with new iron to make more steel. The recycled metal may be turned into another car.

PLASTIC

Oil and gas are the raw materials used for making plastic. Oil is a mixture of many substances which can be separated by evaporation and condensation. There are two major kinds of plastic but they are not easy to recycle.

IN TOUCH WITH THE PAST

Next time you pick up a plastic pen remind yourself that you are holding a material which comes from a substance that formed 200 million years ago. It came from the bodies of tiny plants and animals that lived in the sea. When they died they sank to the sea floor where **micro-organisms** got to work on **decomposing** their bodies. The micro-organisms used oxygen in the water as they fed but they ran out of oxygen before everything had decomposed. The remains formed a thick layer that was buried by sand. In time the sand turned to rock and the remains turned to gas and oil. Today the rocks are drilled to release the gas and oil.

BOILING OIL

Oil is a mixture of substances called **hydrocarbons**. Each one has a different boiling point from the others. They are separated by running hot oil into the bottom of a tall tower. Most of the hydrocarbons evaporate and rise up the tower.

An oil refinery where the hydrocarbons in oil are separated and prepared for making a range of products.

The hydrocarbon **vapour** gets cooler and cooler as it rises and only those hydrocarbons with the lowest boiling points reach the top and are stored as gases. The other hydrocarbons condense at different levels in the tower and are collected separately. The hydrocarbons which condense near the top of the tower are used to make plastics.

Plastics are made into thousands of different products from gloves and brushes to containers of almost any shape.

HARD AND SOFT

There are two kinds of plastic. Thermoplastics are plastics that become soft and melt when they are warmed (like polystyrene cups or perspex sheets). Thermosetting plastics do not melt when heated. They are used for making plastic cases, kitchen working surfaces and table tops. Bakelite ®, melamine and Formica ® are examples of thermosetting plastics.

RECYCLING PLASTIC

Few plastics are easy to recycle. One plastic that can be recycled is called PET, which stands for polythene terephthalate. It is used to make plastic bottles. After the bottles have been collected for recycling they are cleaned, broken down into small pieces and melted to make the plastic ready for shaping and using again.

ROTTING AWAY

You are made up of chemicals which are constantly being recycled. The chemicals in materials made by other living things also recycle quickly and can be put to good use. But the chemicals in some materials may stay where they are for ever.

THE CHEMICAL ROUNDABOUT

You contain more chemicals than a chemistry set. They originally come from water, the air and **minerals** in the soil. Plants make them into food. When you eat a meal your body uses most of them to stay alive and grow. You get rid of the chemicals you do not need as wastes. **Micro-organisms** break down wastes into chemicals which pass back into the air and the soil. When any other living thing dies the micro-organisms break that down too. This recycling of chemicals has been taking place on the Earth for over 3000 million years. Some chemicals in you today may have been in a lettuce last week, and in a 100 years time they may be in a tree.

These potato plants have used the minerals in the compost to make this crop.

WHAT WILL ROT?

A substance such as wood, wool or cotton, which can break down completely to simple chemicals, and which can be used again by living things, is called a **biodegradable** substance. Kitchen wastes such as potato peelings and carrot tops are biodegradable. Iron and steel are not biodegradable because they break down to rust which cannot be used by living things. Nothing rots aluminium or glass.

Almost all plastics are not biodegradable but a biodegradable plastic made from sugar has recently been invented. When you throw it away, micro-organisms break it down into carbon dioxide and water.

USING WASTES

Many gardeners collect up dead plants and micro-organisms rot them down into a substance called compost. Gardeners dig the compost back into the soil. It provides **minerals** for another crop of vegetables or a display of flowers.

In some parts of the world wastes from humans, animals and the kitchen are used to make methane gas, which can be used as a fuel to cook meals. The wastes are stored in pits to rot. As the micro-organisms feed on the wastes they make methane gas. It rises to the top of the pit and is drawn off along a pipe connected to a kitchen stove.

At a rubbish tip materials that will rot are stored with materials that will not rot but could be recycled. Both are being stored uselessly.

HOW RECYCLING HELPS

There is only a certain amount of each type of raw material on Earth. Most raw materials are underground and covered by habitats such as woodlands and rainforests. Energy is needed to manufacture materials and this comes from fuel which is also underground. When materials are thrown away they create environmental problems. Everyone throws away a large amount of rubbish. Recycling could help us and our planet Earth.

SAVING RAW MATERIALS

Each day the amount of raw materials on Earth gets smaller. They are being used up to make the new things we need for our modern way of life. As a raw material becomes scarce it becomes more difficult and more expensive to **extract**. Recycling reduces the amount of a raw material that needs to be extracted. This means it will last longer and will remain cheaper for longer.

SAVING ENERGY

Energy is needed to extract the raw materials and process them to make metals, glass and plastic. Most of the energy comes from fuels which are non-renewable. Recycling material saves fuel because less raw material has to be extracted and processed.

These items are being sorted at a recycling centre. They will be taken away to be made into new products. Some of the new products may find their way back here.

SAVING HABITATS

When raw materials and fuels like coal are extracted, the land above them may be cleared of trees and plants. This allows digging machines to reach them and also makes it easy for trucks to take them away. The habitats of plants and animals are destroyed when land is cleared. Recycling material also saves habitats because there is less need for raw materials and fuel.

A large area of natural habitat has been cleared away to make room for diggers to extract the copper ore in this open-cast mine.

RECYCLING AND RUBBISH

In the past, rubbish has been stored in tips made from disused quarries. As the tips become full new places for waste are needed. Recycling reduces the demand for tipping space and prevents more habitats from being destroyed.

A PILE OF RUBBISH

Every year the people living in your home may produce a tonne of rubbish. If everyone at your school came from a home that produced the same amount of rubbish how many tonnes would the rubbish pile weigh? Imagine that pile of rubbish being produced by the families of everyone in your school every year. Think of the materials that could be recycled and the habitats that could be saved.

THE FUTURE

Our supplies of raw materials will not last for ever but we can make replacements. Recycling now will help prepare for the future. In time our search for new materials may take us beyond the Earth.

WHAT IS LEFT?

The Earth has been searched for all traces of non-renewable materials. The amounts of each one have been calculated. These amounts are based on how long a raw material would last if we used it up as we do now. For example, the amount of aluminium ore left to be mined from places we can easily reach will last for over 200 years. If the ore in places that are difficult to reach is included we have enough aluminium left to last us nearly 800 years. Most other raw materials will not last that long.

USING OUR BRAINS

Humans have existed on this planet for about 2 million years. At first they only used natural materials like stone and renewable ones like wood. It was 8000 years ago that people discovered how to **extract** metal from their ores and in the last 100 years plastics have been developed and widely used. Today there are thousands of materials that have been discovered or invented.

In the future more work will be done to discover ways of using renewable materials instead of non-renewable ones. Plastics are made from oil now, but in future they may be made from plants.

The materials and technology used in the flint axes of the Stone Age.

Although we will eventually run out of the non-renewable materials, we have the intelligence and knowledge of materials to help us replace them.

RECYCLING GIVES US TIME

The human population is expected to reach 10 billion by the end of the 21st century so the demand for materials will continue to increase. Recycling the materials we use today will save more raw materials and fuel for the future and give us longer to prepare for the time when they are used up.

FUTURE AND PAST

The **properties** of stone allowed us to chop wood and the properties of wood allowed us to build homes. Today, the properties of materials we have discovered or invented have allowed us to begin exploring space. In the future we may be able to use raw materials from the Moon or asteroids. By then, people may look back at the materials we use today and think of them as we think of the rocks and pebbles used by our ancestors in the Stone Age. Whatever happens, the material cycle will continue to turn.

The materials in these spacesuits keep the astronauts safe as they repair a satellite brought on board the Space Shuttle.

GLOSSARY

basalt an igneous rock (formed from molten rock beneath the Earth's crust) which cooled quickly and has fine grains

bellows a machine which is used to suck in air and blow it out to increase the temperature of a fire by increasing the speed of burning

biodegradable a property of a material which allows it to be broken down by micro-organisms into simple substances such as water and carbon dioxide

condensation changing from a gas or a vapour into a liquid

conductor a material through which heat or electricity can pass easily

crust the rocky layer which covers the surface of the Earth both on land and beneath the sea

crystal a piece of solid which has flat sides arranged in an orderly way

dam a structure built across a river to prevent the flow of water and to store it in a reservoir

decompose to break down into tiny particles and simple substances

electron microscope a very high powered microscope which uses electrons instead of light to investigate the structure of materials

element a substance which cannot be broken down into simpler substances and is made of only one kind of atom

evaporation changing from a liquid into a gas or a vapour

extract to take out

fibre a very small piece of solid which is long, thin and flexible

furnace a structure in which a large amount of heat can be generated

glacier a huge ice structure made by compacted snow which flows overland and breaks up to form a river or enters the sea

granite an igneous rock (formed from molten rock beneath the Earth's crust) which cooled slowly and has large grains

hydrocarbon a chemical substance made from the two elements hydrogen and oxygen

material a substance which is a solid, liquid or gas

micro-organism a tiny living thing, such as bacteria; it can only be seen with the use of a microscope

mineral a substance in the soil needed by living things or a rocky substance which contains useful materials such as metal

molten the liquid state into which a solid changes when it melts

opaque does not let light pass through

particle a very small piece of a substance

philosopher a person who uses observations and reason to try to understand and explain how things are formed and how they work

pigment small particles, such as those in a powder, that are used to colour an object when made into a paint or ink

plate a large slab of the Earth's rocky crust which moves slowly over the surface of the planet's hot interior

preservative a substance which will stop the decomposition of a material

property a special feature of a material such as its shiny surface or its ability to conduct electricity

pulp mashed up fibres mixed with water

sandstone a rock made by sand grains that have been squashed close together

vapour a kind of gas which easily escapes from the surface of a liquid but condenses back to a liquid when it is cooled

volcano an opening in the Earth's crust through which molten rock, ash and gases come out

volume the amount of space occupied by a substance

weathered where rocks have broken down due to changes in temperature, water and wind

INDEX

HEALTH ISSUES

SMOKING

Sally Morgan

HODDER
Wayland
an imprint of Hodder Children's Books

White-Thomson Publishing Ltd,
2-3 St Andrew's Place, Lewes,
East Sussex BN7 1UP

Published in Great Britain in 2001 by Hodder Wayland, an imprint of Hodder Children's Books.

This book was produced for White-Thomson Publishing Ltd by Ruth Nason.

Design: Carole Binding
Picture research: Glass Onion Pictures

British Library Cataloguing in Publication Data
Morgan, Sally
Smoking. - (Health Issues)
1.Tobacco - Physiological effect 2.Smoking - Health aspects
I. Title
618.2

ISBN 0 7502 3444 X

Printed in Italy by G. Canale & C.S.p.A.

Hodder Children's Books
A division of Hodder Headline Limited
338 Euston Road, London NW1 3BH

Acknowledgements
The author and publishers thank the following for their permission to reproduce photographs and illustrations: John Birdsall Photography: page 21 (library photo); Camera Press: pages 43, 48; Corbis Images: pages 4b, 53 (Duncan Smith); Ecoscene: pages 6 (Christine Osborne), 22 (Christine Osborne), 25 (Chinch Gryniewicz); Angela Hampton Family Life Pictures: pages 19, 20, 22, 47, 52, 55; Peter Newark's American Pictures: page 8; Photofusion: page 54 (Peter Olive); Pictorial Press: pages 16, 45; Popperfoto: pages 14, 28, 49, 59; Chris Schwarz: page 9; Science Photo Library: pages 4t (Bill Barksdale/Agstock), 5 (Oscar Burriel), 35 (Department of Clinical Radiology, Salisbury District Hospital), 39 (Larry Mulvehill), 40 (James Stevenson), 46 (Mark Clarke); Steve Skjold: page 58; Tony Stone Images: pages 7 (Zigy Kaluzny); Topham Picturepoint: pages 12, 17, 18, 44, 57; Wayland Picture Library: pages 10, 13, 23, 26, 30, 32 (Michael Courtney), 37 (Michael Courtney), 38 (Michael Courtney), 50; White-Thomson: page 31t, 31b.

Contents

Introduction
The origins

Tobacco has been smoked, sniffed and chewed for hundreds of years. The tobacco plant originated in North America, where Native Americans used it. Spanish explorers brought tobacco to Europe at the end of the fifteenth century, and its use spread rapidly in some social circles, partly because it was thought to have medicinal value. It was smoked first in pipes and later in cigarettes, which appeared during the mid-nineteenth century and were far more convenient to smoke. This led to an increase in the popularity of smoking, which became a familiar and popular social activity around the world. Today, about one-third of all people aged 15 or over smoke. That's a staggering total of 1.1 billion and the number is still increasing.

Tobacco plants
North Carolina, USA.

'Healing powers'

The Elizabethans were so impressed by the miraculous healing powers of the 'divine tobacco' leaf that they called it herb panacea – the plant to cure all diseases. Native Americans, who had chewed, snorted and smoked tobacco for hundreds of years, believed that tobacco had many medicinal and magical properties. They believed that its powers were greater if it was smoked.

Medicinal uses
Smoking tobacco was advertised to 19th-century New Yorkers as a cure for many respiratory illnesses.

A consumer product that can kill

Smoking is rarely out of the news. Over the last 50 years, thousands of scientific articles have been written showing that smoking causes lung and heart disease, premature death and disability. More recently, there have been campaigns to ban smoking from public places to protect non-smokers from the dangers of inhaling other people's smoke. There are strict regulations relating to the advertising of tobacco products. There are also a number of high-profile court cases in North America and Europe, where people suffering from smoking-related diseases are suing the tobacco companies for damages. And every year there are 'stop smoking' campaigns to help people kick the habit. It's strange to think that tobacco is the only legally available consumer product that kills people when it is used entirely as intended. If cigarettes were invented today, they would be banned immediately.

Heart disease
A modern-day image warns that smoking increases the risk of heart disease.

About this book

Most of you reading this book will be familiar with and relate to the issues covered because you know someone who smokes, are a smoker yourself or are an ex-smoker. Chapter 1 looks at why people start to smoke and how advertising, the media and role models can influence young people. Chapter 2 examines the cigarette itself, the chemicals found in tobacco and their effect on the body, especially the addictive nature of nicotine. In Chapter 3 there is a detailed examination of the effects of smoking on health, and Chapter 4 shows how inhaling someone else's smoke (passive smoking) can harm the health of non-smokers and unborn babies. Chapter 5 considers ways in which a smoker can kick the smoking habit. Sources of information and support are listed on pages 60-61 and the Glossary on page 62 explains less familiar terms.

1 Why smoke? Background, pressures and choices

Increasing numbers of smokers

There are an estimated 1.1 billion smokers in the world, and of these more than 800 million live in developing countries. If the number of people who smoke continues to increase at the current rate, it is predicted that by 2025 there will be a total of 1.64 billion smokers.

The pattern in the increase in the number of smokers around the world is not uniform, however, and there is a distinct difference between developed and developing countries. Between 1981 and 1991, the number of cigarettes smoked fell in developed countries but rose in the developing world. It is still increasing there at a rate of about 3.4 per cent a year.

Malaysia
A group of Malaysian college students relax with cigarettes.

In the UK, the number of smokers peaked in 1972, when almost half of the population smoked. Since then there has been a decline in the number of smokers, especially among older generations. Now smokers make up less than one-third of the population. However, young people are still taking up smoking and replacing older people who are stopping. In contrast, smoking is increasing rapidly in China. Between 1970 and 1992 there, the consumption of cigarettes per adult rose by 260 per cent. There are now about 300 million Chinese smokers, of whom 90 per cent are men.

Teenagers
Some young people smoke as a form of rebellion against the rules at home or at school.

Gender and social class

There are differences in the numbers of male and female smokers. More than one-quarter of smokers in developed countries are women, compared with just one in 14 in developing countries.

There are differences between social classes in all parts of the world. In general, men and women classed as unskilled manual labour are more likely to smoke than people classed as professional. Approximately 12 per cent of men

World cigarette consumption

As you would expect, trillions of cigarettes are smoked each year. In 1998, world production of cigarettes was a massive 5.61 trillion – the equivalent of 948 cigarettes per person or 2.6 cigarettes per day for every man, woman and child.

The largest manufacturer in the world is the state-owned China National Tobacco Corporation, which accounted for one-third of global cigarette production (1.7 trillion cigarettes) in 1997, followed by Philip Morris (USA) and British American Tobacco.

and 11 per cent of women in the professional group smoke, compared with 41 per cent of men and 36 per cent of women in the unskilled manual group.

Why do people smoke?

Given that so many people smoke, there must be some strong reasons for starting. Some of these are:

- to calm their nerves
- to help them during stressful times
- to help them to lose weight
- to give them something to do with their hands
- to make them look cool
- because their friends or family smoke.

There was a surge in the number of smokers during both World Wars. People led incredibly stressful lives in the war years and, not surprisingly, many turned to tobacco. Furthermore, during the Second World War, cigarettes were included in the ration packs of the armed forces. In Europe, the influence of the GIs (American soldiers),

GIs
A war reporter hands cigarettes to US soldiers in Okinawa, Japan, 1945.

most of whom smoked, led to many people taking up the habit. The GIs gave packs of cigarettes along with pairs of silk stockings to their girlfriends. The result was a generation of smokers who, at that time, were unaware of the dangers of smoking to their health.

Teenage smoking

Surprisingly, few adults take up smoking. Most smokers start the habit in their adolescent years. In the UK and the USA, almost one-quarter of 15 year-olds, both boys and girls, are regular smokers. Each day, 3,000 young people (teenagers and younger) in the USA and 450 in the UK smoke their first cigarette. During the 1980s, the number of young people who smoked levelled off and even started to fall, but in the early 1990s there was a sudden upturn that continued until the end of the decade. Then in the UK the numbers fell again, but in the USA they are still rising.

So what encourages a young person to smoke a cigarette for the first time? The three most important factors are parents, siblings and friends. You are three times as likely to smoke if both your parents smoke. Parental opinion is a

Showing the way
A child of parents who smoke is very likely to become a smoker too.

major factor. If you believe that your parents disapprove of smoking, you are less likely to become a smoker. An older brother or sister who smokes also has a strong influence. A younger sibling is more likely to experiment with cigarettes and may even obtain cigarettes from their brother or sister. Friends are the greatest influence in teenage smoking. Teenagers may smoke because they want to belong to a particular group. Others may lack the skills to refuse a cigarette offered by a friend or someone they would like to be their friend.

'There's a small group of smokers at school. They stand in a huddle and pass cigarettes around.' (Claire, 13)

Which children are most likely to become smokers?

A survey of more than 2,000 children aged 12-13 was undertaken in 1988 to predict the onset of smoking. The main factors influencing a young person's decision to smoke are given in order of importance.

Boys

1. having a best friend who smokes
2. knowing at least one cigarette brand
3. having a favourite cigarette advert
4. not knowing or accepting any health risks
5. having at least one parent who smokes

Girls

1. having at least one parent who smokes
2. having positive views about what smoking will do for them; for example, it gives confidence, calms nerves, controls weight
3. knowing at least one cigarette brand
4. having a best friend who smokes
5. not knowing or accepting any health risks

How 9-18 year-olds view smoking

POSITIVE VIEWS	PERCENTAGES OF REGULAR SMOKERS	PERCENTAGES OF NEVER SMOKED
Smoking calms your nerves	72	29
Smoking keeps your weight down	39	17
Smoking gives you confidence	36	10
Smoking is fun	29	1
Smoking makes you feel grown-up	24	24
Smoking makes you look tough	12	20
NEGATIVE VIEWS		
Smoking is a waste of money	75	95
Smoking makes you smelly	63	77
Young people smoke to 'show off'	36	76

Stages in smoking

Young smokers go through a series of stages and each one is influenced by different factors.

1. Precontemplation

The young person is not thinking about smoking, but receives messages about it. At this stage, the person is influenced by their parents, siblings and friends who may smoke, as well as by advertising, smoking in films and on television, and smoking by role models.

'There are always cigarettes lying around our house. One day I was on my own and I tried one.' (Jamie, 14)

2. Contemplation

The influence of friends, family and media build up to a point where curiosity takes over and the young person considers trying a cigarette.

3. Initiation

Most young people will try smoking, but the majority do not become regular smokers. At this stage, friends are usually the strongest influence.

Belonging
Is it necessary to do the same as a group of friends, to feel that you are part of the group?

4. Experimentation

There may be repeated attempts to smoke. Young people can become addicted to nicotine after smoking a very small number of cigarettes, which is why many experimenters become regular smokers. At this stage, peer pressure is still the strongest influence.

5. Regular smoking

This may involve a new set of influences. As well as addiction and habituation, personal factors such as beliefs about the benefits of smoking and self-perception have an effect. Factors such as cost, availability and school policy all play their role.

6. Maintenance

The continuation of regular smoking involves all these influences, but addiction is a major force.

7. Quitting

This occurs when the relative importance of influences changes. A decision to stop can be triggered by, for example, a new non-smoking friend, a steep increase in the price of cigarettes, a decrease in spending money or even working in an office where smoking is not permitted.

Advertising techniques

Advertising can play an important role when a young person makes the all-important decision to smoke his or her first cigarette. Research shows that young people usually smoke the brands that are promoted most heavily. A survey in California in 1996 interviewed just under 1,800 people between the ages of 12 and 17. None of them had ever smoked. When interviewed again three years later, the researchers discovered that 30 per cent had tried a cigarette, 16 per cent were willing to smoke and 3 per cent were smokers. Those who had been able to name a cigarette brand in 1996 were twice as likely to have started, or be willing to start, smoking than those who had not been able to. The three most advertised brands in the USA have a 35 per cent market share. But 86 per cent of underage smokers choose these brands, indicating that young people are heavily influenced by advertising. The importance of advertising to young consumers was evident during 1989 and 1993, when

Adventure

This image appeared on an advertisement for cigarettes which were claimed to have the 'taste of adventure'.

spending on promoting the Joe Camel brand in the USA leapt from $27 million to $43 million. This highly successful campaign resulted in a 50 per cent increase in Camel's share of the youth market. In contrast, it had little impact on the adult market.

Advertising also creates the impression that smoking is a normal, socially acceptable habit. In 1965, cigarette advertising was banned from television in the UK. In 1991, this was extended across the European Union (EU). As a result, cigarette manufacturers started to sponsor sports, such as motor racing, snooker and rugby, as an alternative way of advertising their brands on television. Young people watching these events on television or at the venue cannot miss the advertising posters and banners, and they subconsciously link smoking with the healthy lifestyle associated with sports. One study found that boys whose favourite sport was motor racing were twice as likely to become regular smokers as those who were not interested

Motor racing
Brand names of products (including, sometimes, cigarettes) are displayed on Formula 1 racing cars.

in the sport. Motor racing is one of the few sports that are still allowed to use tobacco sponsorship, but there are plans within the EU to prevent all sponsorship of sports, including Formula 1 racing.

In the USA, tobacco advertisements are also banned from television. In 1998, 46 states signed the Master Settlement Agreement, which bans billboards and restricts outdoor advertising. Recent studies have shown that since 1999, the tobacco companies have dramatically increased their advertising spending in magazines read by large numbers of teenagers.

'Lured in large numbers by the glare and glamour of tobacco marketing that sells a deadly product as the taste of freedom and fashion, between 80,000 and 99,000 children and adolescents in the world take to tobacco every day.' (Dr Gro Harlem Brundtland, head of WHO Tobacco Free Initiative)

Advertising in the press and on posters and other forms of promotion are covered by voluntary agreements. The tobacco companies have agreed that their advertisements will not glamorize smoking or make it appeal to young people, and they will not link smoking with sporting success or make it sexually attractive. However, many people feel that some of the more obscure and puzzling adverts have the effect of making smoking look very sophisticated. There are plans to tighten up the agreements, to restrict the promotion of tobacco at its point of sale in shops, to limit the advertising of tobacco brand names on non-tobacco goods such as boots, flip-flops and baseball caps, and to prohibit the distribution of free cigarettes. Recently, there has been an increase in point-of-sale advertising in the USA, particularly in below-counter-level adverts, which are out of sight for adults but can be seen easily by young children.

Despite the increasing restrictions on tobacco advertising, the amount of money that tobacco companies spend on advertising and promotion has not decreased. The average amount spent each year is approximately $7 billion in the USA – that's a staggering $19 million per day – and £49 million in the UK.

A gentle cigarette
'Some people are known – and loved – for being gentle. So is this cigarette ... especially among our younger smokers' said this advertisement in the 1950s.

New markets

Tobacco companies based in North America and Europe are seeing their home markets shrink. Both the number of smokers and the number of cigarettes smoked per smoker are falling as governments increase taxation on tobacco. Not surprisingly, these companies are turning their attention to the growing markets of East Asian countries, especially South Korea, Taiwan and Japan. The advertising regulations in these countries are not as restrictive, and companies can use many techniques to persuade young people to start smoking. These campaigns can be very effective – tobacco adverts are common along major roads, on the sides of buildings and on television.

According to the World Health Organization (WHO), smoking rates among male Korean teenagers increased from 18 to 30 per cent in the year following the entry of US companies into the market. There was a fourfold increase in smoking among female teenagers. These increases were linked to the massive rise in tobacco advertising and promotion by both US and Korean companies.

In developing countries, just under 50 per cent of men but only 7 per cent of women smoke. So tobacco companies are targeting women. In Sri Lanka, for example, a tobacco company sponsored a 'Golden Tones Disco'. It employed young women in shimmering golden saris to offer each young person entering the disco a free cigarette and a light. Entry to the disco was free for women but men had to pay. Another brand was promoted by women driving around in sports cars handing out free cigarettes. In other countries, advertising campaigns aimed at women have included sponsored fashion collections. The new wave of marketing to women promotes cigarettes with perfumed scents and exotic flavours, and cigarettes with names that include the words 'slims' and 'lights'. Product packaging and advertising have featured watercolours and pastels.

Campaign
Young women are employed to attract attention to cigarettes in Tokyo, Japan.

Smoking and films

The amount of smoking that took place in films declined steadily during the 1960s-80s, but there was an increase in the 1990s. The Dartmouth Medical School study in the USA looked at 603 films between 1988 and 1999 and gauged the level of smoking in each. Researchers then surveyed 5,500 school children at middle school in New Hampshire and Vermont to see if the films affected their smoking habits. The children surveyed were very aware of the smoking that took place in the films and could remember which actors were seen smoking. Those seen smoking most often were Leonardo DiCaprio, Tom Hanks, Julia Roberts and Brad Pitt.

Why do so many girls smoke?

In the past, only a small percentage of girls smoked, but over the last decade this has changed and girls are fast catching up with boys. Teenage girls in the UK are the least likely of all groups to give up smoking.

The big screen
Smoking is often glamorized in films.

So why do girls smoke? This can be summed up in one word: 'image'. Many of their role models, such as fashion models and pop stars, smoke and this can influence young girls' decision to smoke. They understand the warnings on cigarette packs, and realize that their clothes smell and that smoking gives them bad breath, but the lure of smoking is too great. Their boyfriends may influence their smoking habits, and girls are more likely to start smoking if their boyfriends are smokers. Some boys like to see their girlfriends smoke. The effect is greater still if one or both of their parents smoke, and girls are especially influenced by an older brother.

Relationship
Girls may follow their boyfriends in taking up smoking.

As mentioned earlier, there are more female smokers in developed countries than in developing countries. Women in developed countries are more likely to be independent and to have careers, and they are more used to competing with men, especially the younger generations where attitudes associated with 'girl power' are increasingly influential. These attitudes are seen in teenage girls too, as they compete with similar-aged boys at school. In contrast, women in developing countries are more likely to marry young and have to raise a large family.

Saying no

I have never smoked – not even once. When I was at school several of my friends started smoking. We didn't all smoke, but the smokers kept on passing round the pack of cigarettes. They told us that it felt so good to smoke – it gave you a kick, made you feel great. 'Go on – try, it won't bite,' they'd say. Some of their boyfriends smoked too. When we went out together, they would sit at the other end of the table, puffing away, trying to look cool. Fortunately Carole, my best friend, didn't want to smoke either so we stuck it out together. After a while the smokers gave up and left us alone. I think they got bored trying to make us smoke. Now, when I look back, I am so pleased that we didn't give in. I don't think I missed much.
(Sophie, aged 25)

Smoking and mobile phones

There was an unexpected downturn in the number of teenage smokers in the UK during the late 1990s. Between 1996 and 1999, the number of 15-year-old smokers fell from 30 per cent to 23 per cent, a much faster decline than predicted. During the same period, mobile phone ownership increased, with a dramatic rise between 1999 and 2000. By August 2000, more than 70 per cent of 15-17 year-olds owned a phone. Researchers have found that teenagers find mobile phones smart, chic and adult. Teenagers can express their individuality through their choice of brand and model. Peer-group pressure has just as much effect on mobile phone ownership as it does on cigarette smoking. If one member of a group of friends has a mobile phone, then other members will see the phone as essential to socializing. Furthermore, the teenagers buy their phone cards in the same places as they would buy cigarettes. But some cannot afford both, so they have to

Trends

Could the trend for mobile phones contribute to a decline in smoking?

choose between having a mobile phone or smoking. Many teenagers feel that mobile phones, especially the newer models with WAP technology (giving internet access), create a more high-tech image than cigarettes, which are viewed as old technology. More research is currently under way to prove a link between the decline of smoking and the rise of the mobile phone, and research is needed in other parts of the world.

'Mobile phones are marketed in a very similar way to cigarettes with a subtle pitch that focuses on self-image, identity and confidence. The mobile phone makers aren't doing anything wrong, but their advertising is very effective and seductive.' (Anne Charlton, emeritus professor at the University of Manchester)

Selling to children

To prevent children buying cigarettes, many countries have laws that make it illegal for shopkeepers to sell cigarettes to young people. In the UK, the minimum age for buying tobacco is 16. In the USA, the majority of states have a minimum age of 18, with the exception of Alabama, Alaska and Utah, which have a minimum age of 19, and Pennsylvania, which has a minimum age of 21. In both countries, shopkeepers can be prosecuted if they are found to have sold cigarettes to underage customers. Some US states are applying penalties to children caught in possession of tobacco, as a means of discouraging under-age smoking. The penalites include carrying out a specific number of hours of community service and having your driving licence suspended.

'I spend my spare time mucking around with my computer. If I smoked I wouldn't have enough money to buy computer games and new kit.' (Mark, 14)

2 What's in a cigarette? The main ingredients

Cigarettes are made from tobacco. The tobacco leaves are harvested, dried and transported to factories, where the tobacco is finely chopped and rolled up within a paper case, then cut to length. Different brands of cigarettes taste different, depending on the source of the tobacco, the amount of tar in the tobacco, and the additives that are mixed in with the tobacco by the cigarette manufacturers. The tobacco is blended for aroma, taste and character to meet smokers' preferences.

Harvesting
Tobacco leaves are harvested on a plantation in Cuba.

Three types of tobacco are used in cigarettes: Virginia or flue-cured, burley and oriental. Smokers' tastes vary considerably around the world. In the UK, people prefer the Virginia tobaccos, whereas in the USA, they prefer a blend of all three types of tobacco.

Nowadays, all cigarettes have filters that are located at the 'mouth-end' of the cigarette. The filter reduces the amount of smoke that reaches the smoker. Most filters are made from cellulose fibres. The filter has no taste and is firm enough to hold its shape. Different kinds of filters deliver different amounts of tar and nicotine.

The cigarette manufacturer can control the amount of air that enters the cigarette as it is smoked. This is called ventilation. A cigarette can be ventilated to dilute the smoke, which in turn reduces the amount of tar, nicotine and carbon monoxide reaching the smoker. All cigarettes are ventilated by the paper, through which air can penetrate, and many are also ventilated through small air holes in the filter tip. When a smoker inhales, air is drawn in through these small holes and mixes with air drawn in through the lit end, diluting the smoke. Filter ventilation is a particularly important feature of lower-tar cigarettes.

What's in smoke?

When a cigarette is lit, it starts to burn and releases smoke. When a smoker inhales, the smoke is drawn along the cigarette and through the filter, and from there into the mouth.

Smokescreen
Side-stream smoke pollutes the atmosphere around a smoker.

The smoke that enters the lungs of the smoker is called main-stream smoke. It is smoke that is formed and inhaled when the smoker 'puffs'. Side-stream smoke forms when the cigarette smoulders between puffs. The smoker never inhales this smoke. As much as 85 per cent of cigarette smoke in a room comes from side-stream smoke.

Tobacco contains approximately 2,500 different compounds. When it burns, many more are formed. Analysis indicates that there may be as many as 4,000 different chemical compounds in tobacco smoke, some of which have been proved to be harmful. Many potentially toxic gases are present in higher concentrations in side-stream smoke than in main-stream smoke.

The smoke contains tiny particles of tar (which is itself composed of many chemicals), nicotine, benzene and benzo(a)pyrene as well as carbon monoxide, ammonia, dimethyl-nitrosamine, formaldehyde and hydrogen cyanide in gaseous form. Some of these chemicals have irritant properties and 60 or so may be carcinogens, or cancer-forming substances. The effects of some of the main components of cigarette smoke are discussed below.

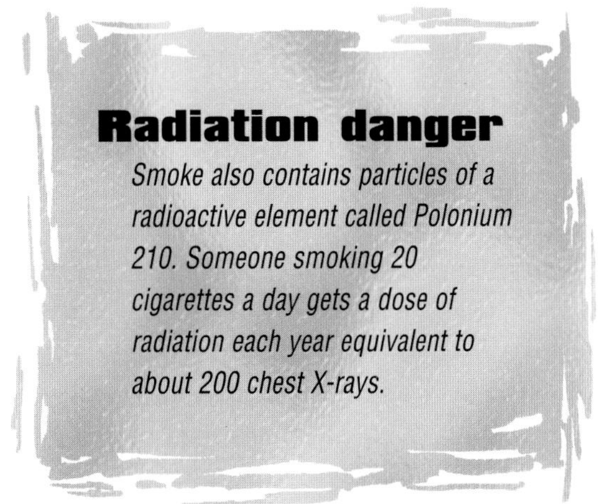

Radiation danger

Smoke also contains particles of a radioactive element called Polonium 210. Someone smoking 20 cigarettes a day gets a dose of radiation each year equivalent to about 200 chest X-rays.

Nicotine

Nicotine is the main compound present in tobacco. It is colourless but poisonous. In fact, nicotine has long been used as a pesticide to kill insects. If the nicotine content of one cigarette were injected straight into the body it would be fatal, but it is non-lethal if inhaled.

Nicotine is a powerful drug that can affect every organ in the body. It takes just seven seconds for the nicotine in cigarette smoke to reach the brain, where it causes the release of a chemical called dopamine. Dopamine creates pleasurable sensations and can change a person's mood. Nicotine has many effects on the body, but the most important one is to stimulate the release of a hormone, adrenalin. This is often described as the flight or fight hormone. When you suddenly find yourself in a stressful situation, such as being frightened or being attacked by something or someone, adrenalin is released. It increases your heart rate and blood pressure and affects your nervous system, preparing you for running or fighting. You have probably noticed that if you are suddenly frightened your heart starts pounding – this is caused by adrenalin. The effects of adrenalin are the same, whether stimulated by a stress or by smoking.

'Smoking helps me to relax after a stressful day in the office. Within seconds of inhaling, I feel a sense of calm and I can unwind.' (Alex, office worker)

Nicotine is addictive. Soon after smoking a cigarette, the brain starts to want more nicotine. Many people begin to feel increasingly uncomfortable until they have their next cigarette. Smoking feels pleasurable, but much of the pleasure of smoking is the relief from the withdrawal effects of nicotine. Many people feel distracted or unable to enjoy themselves when they are unable to smoke. One measure of addiction is how long after waking a person smokes their first cigarette of the day. In 1998, 31 per cent of smokers had their first cigarette within 15 minutes of waking. Young people who experiment with cigarettes quickly become addicted to the nicotine in tobacco, and they have similar levels of nicotine dependence as adults. Many teenagers who smoke light their first cigarette within 30 minutes of waking up. It is the addiction to nicotine that makes it difficult, but not impossible, for people to stop smoking, and there are unpleasant withdrawal symptoms (see page 53).

Addiction
It is nicotine that makes a smoker follow one cigarette with another.

Carbon monoxide

Carbon monoxide is a deadly gas. It has no smell, and when it enters the bloodstream it can have serious effects. Normally, oxygen passes from the air in the lungs into the blood capillaries of the lungs. It is picked up by a molecule called haemoglobin, which is found in red blood cells. The red blood cells carry the oxygen to the tissues and organs of the body, where it is released. If carbon monoxide is present in the blood, red blood cells pick up this gas in preference to the oxygen. Therefore less oxygen is carried by the red blood cells and less reaches the rest of the body. Having a small quantity of carbon monoxide in the blood can make a person feel tired and lacking in energy. In time, the regular presence of carbon monoxide in the blood leads to a thickening of the arteries, especially the coronary arteries supplying oxygen to the heart (see page 37).

The burning of petrol in car engines also releases carbon monoxide, but modern cars are fitted with devices to remove this gas. There is no such device fitted on a cigarette, although the technology exists to modify a cigarette filter to absorb carbon monoxide.

Tar

Tar is a sticky brown substance that is produced when tobacco is burnt. It stains the fingers, teeth and tongue of the smoker. It coats everything with which it comes into contact, especially the tiny hairs called cilia that line the trachea and bronchi (see page 33). Tar collects in the lungs and builds up over a number of years, staining the lung tissue. The presence of tar in the lungs is one of the main causes of lung cancer.

Tar
A health campaign poster showed this image of the amount of tar that collects in an average smoker's lungs.

Hydrogen cyanide

Tobacco smoke contains the gas hydrogen cyanide. This causes headaches, dizziness, weakness, nausea, vertigo and stomach aches in both smokers and non-smokers.

Additives

A number of additives are mixed with tobacco during the manufacturing process. Before 1970, few additives were used in the manufacture of tobacco products; now more than 600 can be used. Manufacturers state that additives are used for a particular purpose. For example, food-type ingredients and flavourings can balance the natural tobacco taste, replace the sugars lost in the drying process and give individual brands their characteristic flavour and aroma. Other additives have technological functions, such as controlling moisture, protecting against microbial degradation and acting as binders or fillers.

However, many anti-smoking groups claim that some additives have a different purpose: they are used to make the cigarette more addictive or more appealing to new smokers. There are additives on the permitted list that enhance the addictive 'kick' that smokers experience when they smoke the cigarette. For example, ammonium compounds increase the alkalinity of smoke in order to increase the amount of nicotine that is released. Some additives are used to enhance the taste of tobacco smoke to make the product more attractive to consumers. Sweeteners and chocolate may help to make cigarettes more palatable to first-time users. Eugenol and menthol numb the throat, so smokers cannot feel the irritating effects of the smoke as it passes into their lungs. Cocoa may be used to dilate, or enlarge, the tubes into the lungs so that the smoke can pass more quickly and more deeply into the lungs. This enables more nicotine to pass into the bloodstream. Other additives mask the smell and visibility of side-stream smoke. This makes it difficult for other people to detect the smoke and thus weakens the claims of non-smokers that smoking is anti-social.

There is considerable debate about the role of additives. Cigarette manufacturers dispute claims that additives are responsible for the increase in smoking. There are laws that control which additives may be used in cigarette manufacture. All the permitted additives must be tested for direct toxicity. This means the individual additive is tested to see if it has any toxic effect on humans. Unfortunately, when cocktails of additives are burnt, new products of combustion are formed and these may be toxic. However, manufacturers are not required to state which additives they have used in their cigarettes. This means that smokers have no way of knowing whether the brand they smoke contains any or many additives.

A manufacturer's view

A statement from British Amcrican Tobacco says:

'ingredients are not added to increase the amount of nicotine in cigarette smoke. Tobacco products are not "spiked" with nicotine. Ingredients do not make it easier for people to start smoking, or influence a decision to quit. Ingredients are not added to make cigarettes appealing to children, and there is no evidence whatsoever that they have this effect. ... sugars, cocoa and fruit extracts ... do not create a sweet, chocolate-like or fruity taste in the smoke. They blend with tobacco, making a characteristic tobacco taste distinct from the effect these ingredients have in foods.'

3 Smoking and your health
Effects on the body

The first warning signs that smoking was harming people's health emerged in the 1930s when doctors noticed an increase in lung diseases such as emphysema and lung cancer. Since the 1950s, more than 70,000 scientific articles have shown that prolonged smoking causes premature death and disability. Today, smoking is a major cause of death throughout the world.

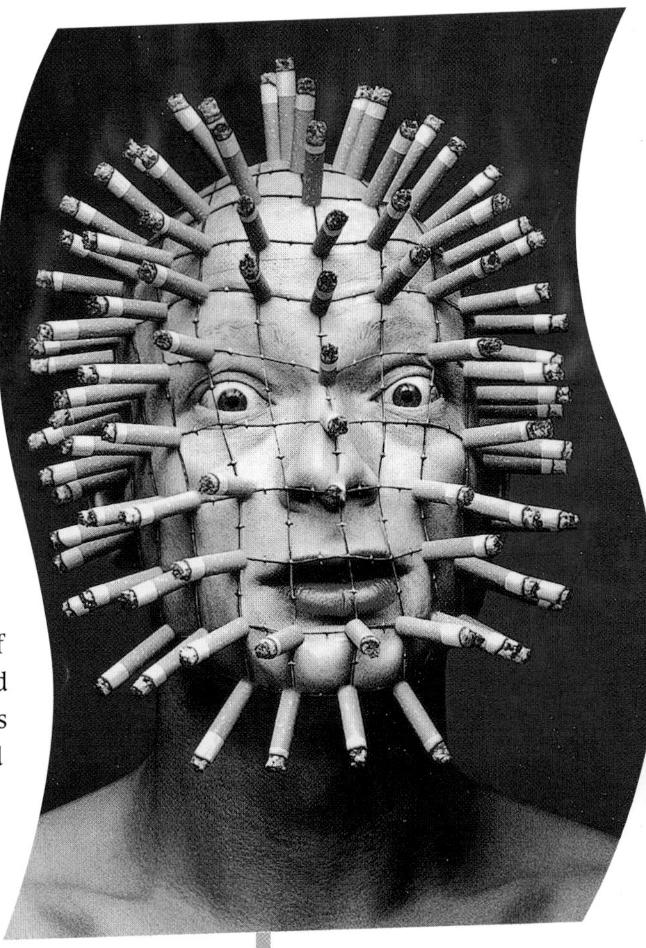

Dutch warning
A poster produced by the anti-smoking campaign in the Netherlands.

A worldwide cause of death

In the 50 years between 1950 and 2000, an estimated 6 million Britons and 60 million people in the rest of the world died from tobacco-related diseases. The annual death rate is currently about 4 million, divided equally between developed and developing countries. Each year, approximately 500,000 people in the USA die prematurely as a result of smoking-related diseases. A similar number die in the EU, including more than 120,000 in the UK – that's about 330 a day or the same as a jumbo jet crashing and killing all its passengers. In China, there are nearly 1 million deaths each year, and this figure is expected to double by 2025. Some scientists estimate that during the 21st century, the total number of deaths from a smoking-related cause could be as high as 1 billion. By 2030, smoking will probably be the single biggest cause of death in the world, causing about one in three of all adult deaths. More than two-thirds of these will be in the developing world.

Lung cancer is probably the best-known disease linked with smoking. During the 1930s a number of doctors reported a rapid rise in lung cancer, which was once a rare disease, among smokers. In 1950, Sir Richard Doll, a leading cancer epidemiologist in the UK, published a paper that first established a link between smoking and lung cancer. Originally, he thought that the lung cancer was linked to the fumes produced by the increasing number of cars, but further analysis showed that tobacco was the culprit. However, smoking doesn't just cause lung cancer. It has been linked to many other diseases, such as bronchitis, coronary heart disease and even blindness.

In countries where cigarette smoking has been common for several decades, smoking in people aged 35-69 accounts for:

- about 90 per cent of all lung cancer cases
- 15-20 per cent of other cancers
- 75 per cent of chronic bronchitis and emphysema
- 25 per cent of deaths from cardiovascular diseases.

In developing countries, smoking is more likely to cause chronic respiratory diseases than cancer and cardiovascular disease.

Increased risk

People who smoke are more likely than non-smokers to suffer from these conditions:

Severe circulatory disease
Angina (20 x rick)
Peripheral vascular disease
Stomach and duodenal ulcers
Influenza
Pneumonia
Cataract (2 x risk)
Loss of vision
Abnormal eye movements
Fungal eye infection
Macular degeneration (eyes, 2 x risk)
Acute necrotizing ulcerative gingivitis (gum disease) and tooth loss
Colon polyps
Crohn's disease (chronic inflamed bowel)
Osteoarthritis
Osteoporosis (in both sexes)
Inability to have an erection
Impotence (2 x risk)
Depression
Tuberculosis
Hearing loss
Diabetes
Psoriasis (2 x risk)
Skin wrinkling (2 x risk)
Tendon and ligament injuries
Muscle injuries

Symptoms worse

The symptoms of the following are worse for smokers than non-smokers:

Asthma
Graves' disease (over-active thyroid gland)
Chronic rhinitis (chronic inflammation of the nose)
Multiple sclerosis
Diabetic retinopathy (eyes)
Optic neuritis (eyes)

Saying no
Remembering the physical problems that smoking can cause may make it easier to say no.

There is a wide range of little-publicized health problems associated with smoking. It can affect your senses of taste and smell. Smokers are more likely to develop facial wrinkles at a younger age and have dental hygiene problems. Stomach ulcers are made worse by smoking, and wounds, including surgical incisions, in smokers take longer to heal. Teenage smokers experience more asthma and respiratory symptoms than non-smokers, suffer poorer health, have more school absences and are less fit.

Functions impaired

Smoking affects the following body functions:

Immune system (impaired)
Ejaculation (volume reduced)
Sperm count reduced
Sperm shape abnormalities increased
Sperm motility impaired
Sperm less able to penetrate the ovum
Menopause (onset 1.74 years early on average)
Fertility (30 per cent lower in women)

Fitness
The pleasure of feeling fit is another argument for not smoking.

The immediate effects of smoking include:

- changes in blood vessels
- lower resistance to infection
- higher levels of carbon monoxide, leading to a lack of energy
- damage to the cilia lining the trachea and bronchial tubes, allowing more mucus, dirt and germs to accumulate in the lungs
- bronchitis
- more frequent coughs, colds, earache, sore throats and other minor ailments.

'Jogging, swimming and tennis help to keep us fit. Being fit is important to us. Exercise burns off the calories so we can eat more without worrying about putting on weight! We can't imagine what it must be like not to be fit.' (Layla, Anna and Stephanie, 14)

Smoking and your lungs

The first symptom of lung damage is the classic smoker's cough – an irritating cough that smokers experience first thing in the morning. It clears the lungs of accumulated mucus. The damage gets worse and progresses to more serious diseases such as bronchitis and emphysema and lung cancer.

Working lungs

When you inhale your ribs rise up and out and your diaphragm (the sheet of muscle between your chest and abdomen) flattens. This increases the volume of the chest, pulling air into the lungs. The air rushes down the trachea (windpipe) and into two large tubes called bronchi (one bronchus per lung).

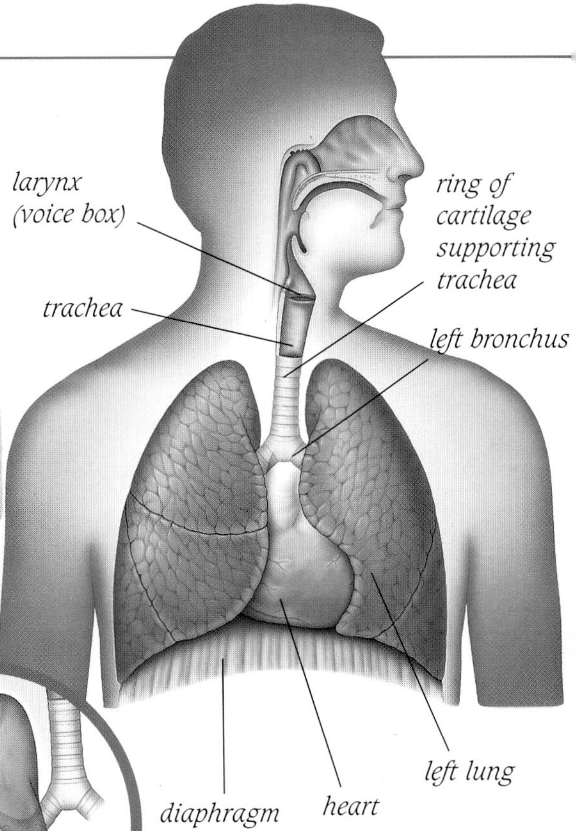

Inside right lung

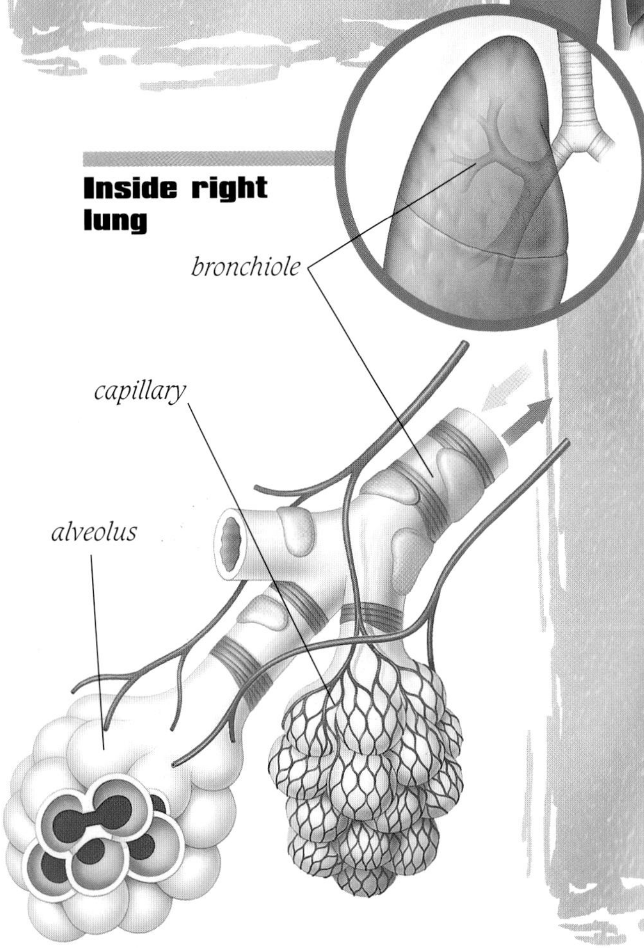

The bronchi divide many times, forming narrower and narrower tubes that eventually end in sacs called alveoli. Gas exchange takes place in the alveoli. The alveoli are surrounded by tiny blood vessels called capillaries. Oxygen in the inhaled air passes through the thin wall of the alveolus into the capillary, where it is picked up by red blood cells. Carbon dioxide leaves the blood and passes into the alveoli. When you exhale the ribs relax, the diaphragm returns to a domed shape and the air is expelled from the lungs.

Inside your lungs

The trachea and the bronchi are lined with tiny hairs called cilia. The cilia are covered with a protective layer of mucus. Germs and dirt become trapped in the mucus, which is swept upwards by the cilia into the throat and swallowed. But the chemicals in tobacco smoke paralyse the cilia, allowing mucus to build up in the lungs. The presence of tar in the lungs stimulates the cells to produce even more mucus. A smoker has to cough to clear the mucus. The build-up of mucus can lead to bronchitis, a condition in which the trachea and bronchi become inflamed. The tubes swell up and breathing becomes difficult. Many people experience *acute* bronchitis when a cold or flu goes to the chest and they have a wheezy cough that clears up after a few days. Smokers suffer from *chronic* bronchitis, a progressive disease that kills thousands each year.

Emphysema

Emphysema is a long-term chronic condition affecting the lungs. Continual coughing damages the alveoli and several sacs may join together. This means there are fewer, larger sacs and a reduced surface area of the lungs through which oxygen can be absorbed. The walls of the alveoli become less elastic, so they do not stretch and recoil as the lungs inflate and deflate. The lack of elasticity makes it difficult to force air from the lungs when breathing out. Sufferers cannot oxygenate the body properly and they become breathless and exhausted after the slightest exercise. Unfortunately, there is no cure. Eventually, sufferers become bed-bound and have to use facemasks to get sufficient oxygen into the lungs.

Teaching with emphysema

I smoked 20 cigarettes a day for 20 years before giving up. I have emphysema now. My lungs are slowly getting worse. I can't sit in a smoky room because it affects my lungs. I find it difficult to take in enough breath to raise my voice so that pupils at the back can hear. It is very tiring to stand up and walk around a room for the duration of a lesson. Imagine having a strap around your chest and then trying to breathe in. You find you can't get enough air into your lungs – that's how I feel most of the time. Once we did a class experiment when pupils found out their lung capacity by blowing into a special bag. One or two of the pupils sang in the school choir and they had a really good lung capacity of 5 litres. Most had a lung capacity of about 4 litres. Mine was barely 2 litres. (John, teacher)

Lung cancer

Lung cancer is the most common form of cancer in the world. Approximately 165,000 new cases were diagnosed in the USA in 2000, and in the same year more than 157,000 Americans died from lung cancer. In the UK, approximately 35,000 people die from the disease each year. Most of the new cases are people in their 60s and 70s who started smoking during and after the Second World War.

Fortunately, the number of deaths is beginning to decline as more people give up smoking. Fewer men are suffering from lung cancer, but now there are more women smokers an increasing number of women are diagnosed with this disease. In Europe and North America, more women die from lung cancer than from breast cancer.

Carcinogens

A large number of substances are known to cause cancers. They are called carcinogens. They include the tar in tobacco smoke, benzene and even dietary supplements. Exposure to ultraviolet light, radioactivity and X-rays can cause cells to become cancerous. Some people have genes that make them more vulnerable to cancer.

Cancer is an uncontrollable growth of cells. Something alters a cell's genes so that the cell divides over and over again, creating an irregular mass of cells called a tumour. By the time a tumour is detected there may be 1,000 million cells present. The genes that cause the cancer are called oncogenes. These are genes that were once responsible for normal cell division but have been changed in some way so that they no longer function properly. Cancer cells live longer than other cells and disrupt the normal functioning of tissues and organs. Sometimes, a few cells break away from the main tumour and are carried in the bloodstream to other parts of the body to form secondary tumours. Many cancers are malignant, which means that they will spread and eventually kill the sufferer.

'It's not just older people who get lung cancer. I had to tell a 37 year-old man that he had lung cancer. He had a wife and two teenage children. He was devastated.'
(Anthony, family doctor)

Lung cancer is difficult to detect in the early stages. It can take two years for a grape-sized clump of cancer cells to form. Most symptoms, such as a persistent cough, pains in the chest, breathlessness and coughing up bloodstained mucus, only appear when the tumour is large enough to interfere with breathing. Unfortunately, some of these symptoms are similar to those that smokers experience normally, so they ignore them. A large tumour can block a bronchus or a major bronchiole. This stops the air flowing into the lungs and causes blood vessels to bleed.

Lung cancer
This coloured X-ray shows an oval-shaped tumour in a person's left lung.

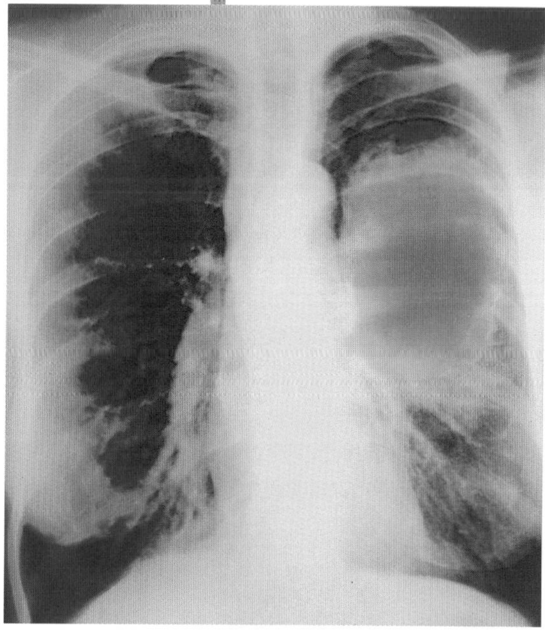

Most cancers are detected by an X-ray
On an X-ray film the tumour appears as a shadow in the chest cavity. Doctors may look inside the lungs using a tube

Surviving lung cancer

I was 49 when I was diagnosed with cancer in my right lung. The lung needed to be removed. Before operating on my lung, the surgeon removed some lymph nodes from my neck and carried out a biopsy to see if the cancer had spread. Well, it had. There was cancer in one lymph node. So he quickly closed me up. I was told I needed chemotherapy and radiation. I received three treatments of chemo over the next few months. It meant sitting for five hours while they pumped me full of the drug. I couldn't sleep for the first few days and I would hurt very badly for a day. And, of course, my hair fell out. They had to be careful when they gave me radiation, as the tumour was near my heart. Once my oesophagus was burnt and they had to squirt liquid painkiller down my throat just so that I could drink water. After 45 radiation treatments I was sent for a scan which showed that the tumour had shrunk and there was no cancer anywhere else in my body. I had an operation to remove my right lung and all the surrounding lymph nodes. I was declared cancer-free. It was painful for a couple of months, but I kept getting better and regained my weight. At my 3-month check-up they did CAT scans, TBCs and a liver function test, and found nothing.

called an endoscope or give the patient a CT scan, which produces a much more detailed image of the chest. The cancer can be treated in a number of ways. Small cancers can be surgically removed. Sometimes a whole lung is removed to ensure a cure. Some patients receive radiotherapy, where strong X-rays are directed at the tumour to kill the cells. Chemotherapy makes use of powerful drugs to kill the cancerous cells. Despite all the advances in cancer treatments, 75 per cent of all people diagnosed with lung cancer die of the disease, with fewer than 10 per cent of patients surviving five years after diagnosis. This is because the cancer spreads through the bloodstream before the first tumour is even detected.

Overall, up to 20 per cent of all cancer deaths can be linked to smoking. Smoking is connected with cancers of the mouth, lip, throat, stomach, pancreas, bladder, kidney, liver and cervix as well as leukaemia (a cancer that affects the white blood cells).

The risks

The risk of contracting lung cancer depends on how many cigarettes are smoked each day and over how many years.

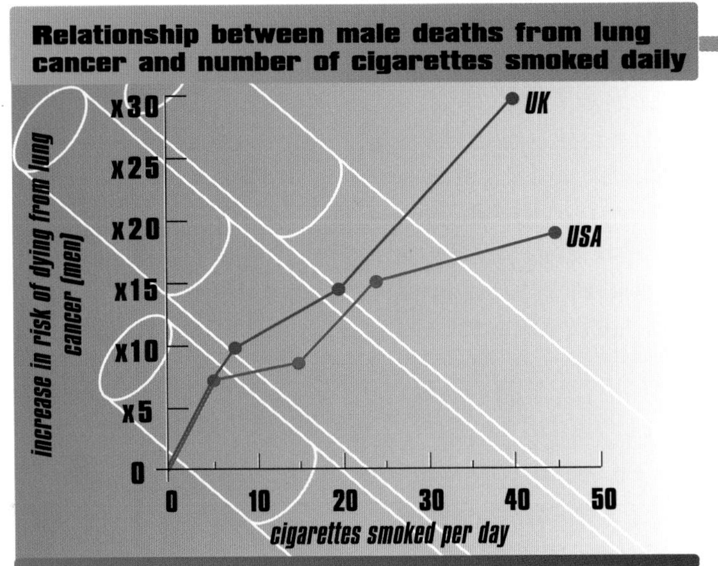

Smoking and lung cancer
The more cigarettes a person smokes, the greater his or her risk of death from lung cancer.

A person who smokes 1-14 cigarettes per day has eight times more risk of dying from lung cancer than a non-smoker; a person who smokes more than 25 cigarettes per day has 15 times more risk. The number of years that a person has been a smoker is even more important than the number of cigarettes. The longer a person smokes, the greater is the risk of getting lung cancer. For example, smoking one packet of cigarettes per day for 40 years increases the risk of lung cancer by eight times compared with smoking two packets per day for 20 years. Approximately 16 per cent of men who smoke throughout their adult life until they are 75 years old will get lung cancer – that's if another smoking-related disease, such as heart disease, doesn't kill them first. However, the risk of contracting lung cancer starts to fall as soon as the person gives up smoking.

The incidence of lung cancer is also linked to social class. For example, men in the 15-64 age group who are manual and factory workers are three times as likely to contract lung cancer as professional men.

Coronary arteries in the heart

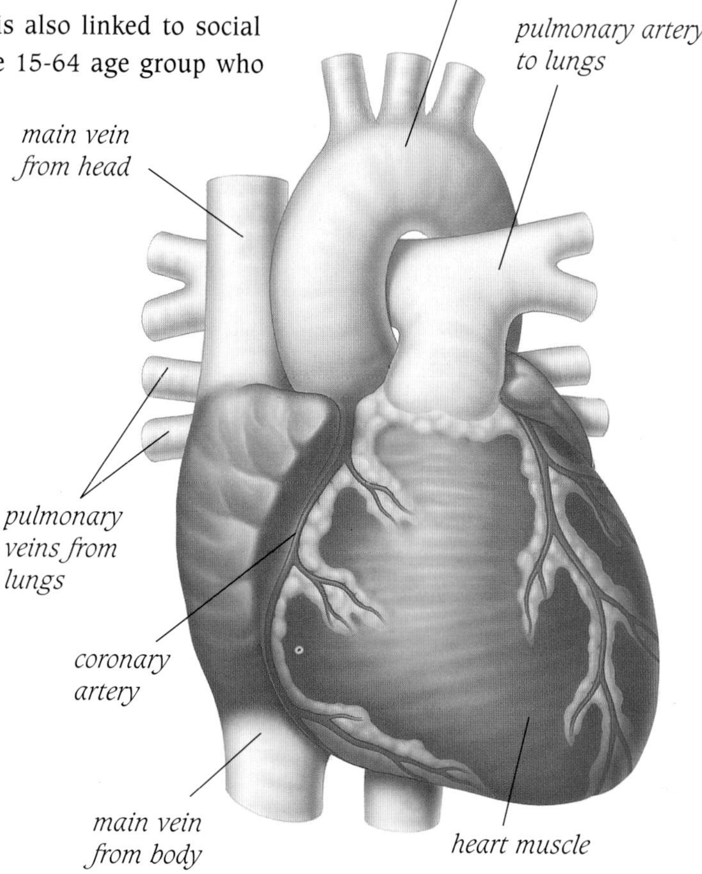

Smoking and the blood circulation

Coronary heart disease is a leading cause of death in most developed countries, and about one-quarter of these deaths can be linked to smoking. Smoking increases the risk of having a heart attack by two or three times.

As a person gets older, fatty deposits are laid down in patches on the lining of major arteries. The deposits become more frequent and larger. Some patches may join up and cause an artery to become narrower, which restricts the blood flow along the artery. It's a bit like furring of the pipes. The heart has to pump harder to get the blood through. However, there are no symptoms until a major artery is affected.

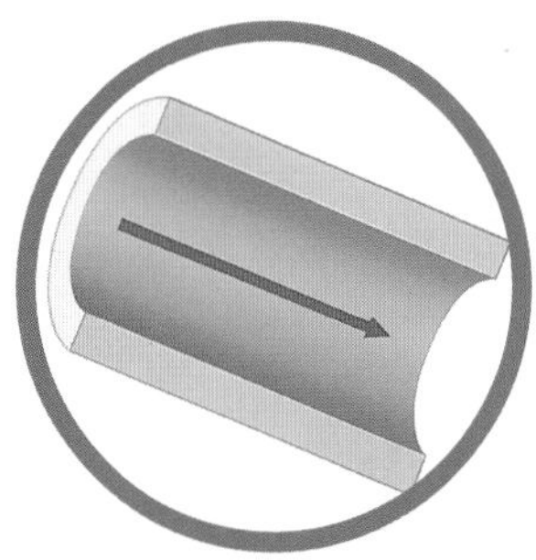
blood flow through normal artery

The coronary arteries supply the heart muscle with oxygenated blood. Any blockage in these arteries would reduce the supply of oxygenated blood to the heart. Sometimes, the surface of the fatty deposits becomes rough and this causes a blood clot, or thrombus, to form. If this occurs in a coronary artery, the clot blocks the artery completely, starving the heart of oxygen and causing a heart attack. Unless the person gets medical treatment straight away, they are likely to die. A person may get an early warning when the coronary arteries become partially

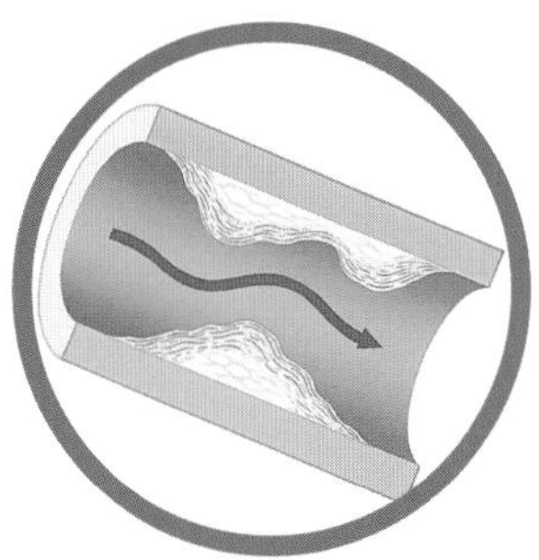
blood flow through artery with fatty deposits

Having a heart attack

David was driving to work when he felt a twinge of pain in his chest and dizziness. He pulled to the side of the road and got out of his car. He started to sweat heavily and found he could not swallow. The pain spread across his chest and down his left arm. He was having a heart attack. He flagged down a passing driver who called for an ambulance. After his arrival at hospital David was attached to an electrocardiogram to monitor his heart and given a diamorphine injection to relieve the pain. He was also given an injection of a clot-busting drug. This breaks down the clot that has formed in the arteries, allowing more blood to flow through. If given soon after the onset of the heart attack, it can save a person's life. He had some blood tests and an X-ray. David spent a week in hospital before being allowed home. He was given beta-blockers to reduce the likelihood of another attack and told to take aspirin, which helps to prevent the clots re-forming. It was 12 weeks before he was fit enough to return to work. He is now on the road to recovery. He has stopped smoking and changed his diet.

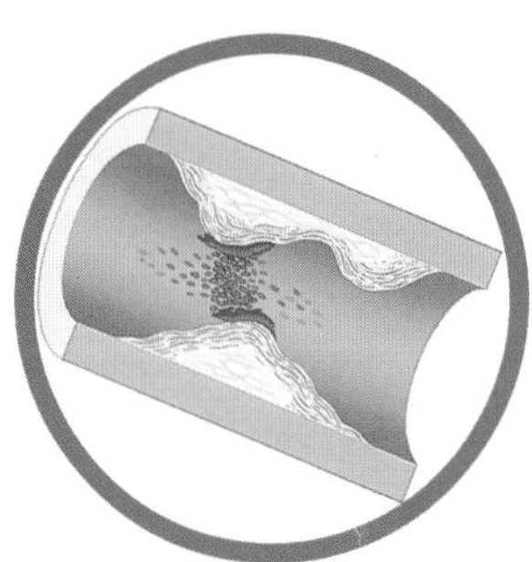
formation of blood clot

blocked. They may suffer from chest pains during or after exercise. This condition is called angina. Angina can be treated, but it is a warning that the person is at risk from a heart attack. A person with furred-up coronary arteries can have coronary bypass surgery. This is when the blocked section of a coronary artery is replaced by a length of vein taken from the patient's leg.

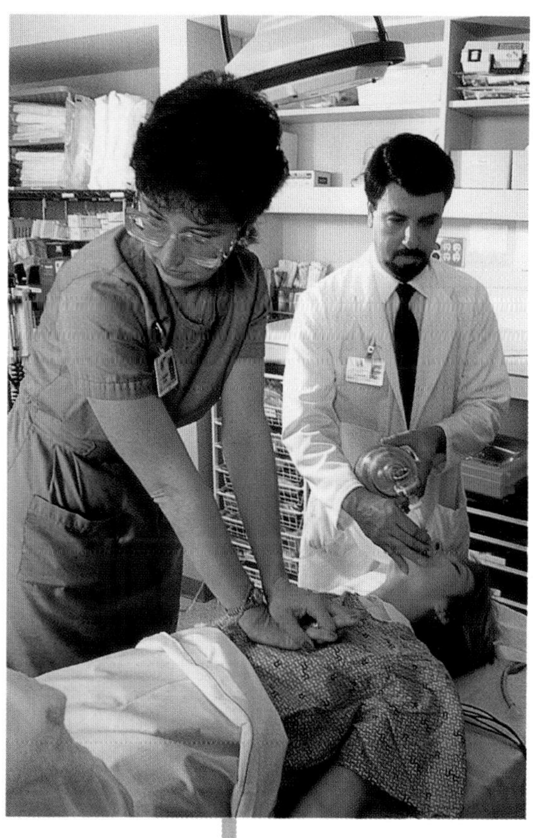

Heart attack
Cardiac massage and giving oxygen through a face mask are two life-saving treatments.

The incidence of heart disease has increased dramatically over the last 50 years, suggesting that the causes of the disease are linked to lifestyle. The main factors are fatty diets, stress, lack of exercise and smoking. The nicotine and carbon monoxide from smoke increase the tendency of blood to clot and this adds to the blockage in the arteries. The carbon monoxide increases the rate at which the fatty deposits are laid down.

It's not just the heart that can be affected by smoking. The blood vessels of the legs and arms, known as the peripheral circulation, can also be harmed. One unpleasant condition is peripheral vascular disease, which can result in the amputation of one or both legs. The arteries supplying the arms and legs become narrower as fatty deposits build up. The person experiences leg pain in the calf muscles when walking or taking exercise. As the arteries become narrower, the pain gets worse. Eventually, there is so little blood flow to the leg that the skin and other tissues die and gangrene, a type of infection, sets in. Doctors have to amputate the leg to prevent the infection spreading and becoming life-threatening. Smoking causes approximately 90 per cent of cases of peripheral vascular disease. In the UK, there are about 2,000 amputations each year.

Strokes

If the blood flow through the arteries supplying the brain is restricted, part of the brain can become starved of oxygen. This causes the brain cells to die and the person is said to have had a stroke. This can result in loss of function or sensation associated with the part of the brain that was starved of oxygen. Smoking causes an increase in blood pressure and this increases the risk of a stroke.

Smoking and the reproductive organs

Smoking can affect sperm production in men and menstruation in women. Smoking in men has been associated with a reduced sperm count, increased sperm abnormalities and impotence (an inability to have an erection owing to decreased blood flow to the penis). Smoking in women has been linked to an increased likelihood of menstrual problems and an earlier menopause (the cessation of menstruation). On average, women smokers go through the menopause up to two years earlier than non-smokers and have a greater risk of developing osteoporosis (see page 41).

Tar stains

As well as affecting the texture of the skin, smoking gradually stains the hand that holds the cigarettes.

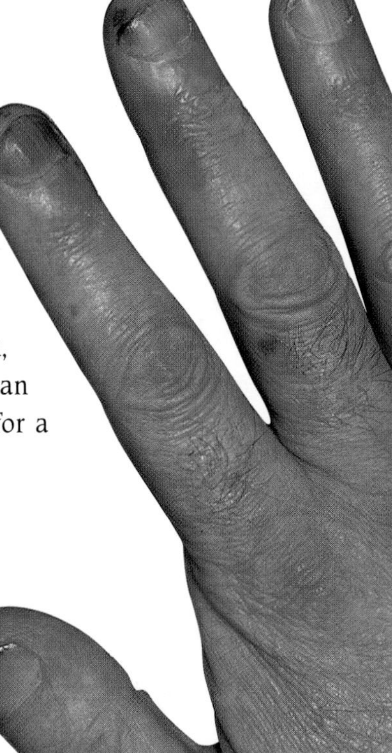

The most common and reliable form of contraception is the pill, which is taken daily for 21 days each month. Each pill contains a dose of female reproductive hormones that is sufficient to prevent the woman from ovulating and becoming pregnant. One of the side effects of the contraceptive pill, especially if taken over a long time, is an increased risk of a heart attack, stroke or other cardiovascular disease. If a woman smokes as well, the risk is 10 times greater than for a non-smoking woman who takes the pill.

Smoking and your skin

For most people, looking good is important. But smoking can have long-term effects on the skin and cause premature ageing. The smoke damages the skin's structure by destroying the collagen, one of the structural components in skin. The collagen fibres give support to the skin and keep it firm. When collagen is damaged, the skin loses its elasticity and becomes leathery. The result is wrinkles, especially around the eyes and mouth. The tar in cigarette smoke often gives the complexion an ash-grey colour. By the time a regular smoker reaches the age of 40, their skin condition is more like that of someone 20 years older.

Smoking and osteoporosis

Osteoporosis is a disease that affects older people, especially women. The slow loss of bone mineral density causes the bones to become brittle and more liable to fractures. When an older women falls, osteoporosis makes it more likely that she will fracture her hip. Although a hip fracture can be repaired, it can cause some degree of disability. Researchers have found that the bones of smokers lose calcium at a greater rate than the bones of non-smokers. Consequently, as many as one in every eight hip fractures could be the result of smoking.

'I can't believe the number of models who smoke. They spend a fortune on skin products and then they ruin it all by smoking. Don't they realize what they are doing to their skin? By the time they are 30 their face will be too wrinkled for this business.' (Rachel, make-up artist)

Health warnings

In 1966, the US government passed laws requiring cigarette manufacturers to place this warning on all their cigarette packets: 'Caution: smoking may be hazardous to health'. This had to appear on all advertising from 1972. Over the years the warning has changed, and now there are several different phrases that manufacturers must use.

The EU requires the manufacturer to place a general warning 'Tobacco seriously damages health' on the most visible surface of a cigarette pack, together with a second warning on the next largest surface. This could be any one of the following:

- Smoking causes cancer
- Smoking causes heart disease
- Smoking causes fatal diseases

- Smoking kills
- Smoking can kill
- Smoking when pregnant harms your baby
- Protect children: don't make them breathe your smoke
- Smoking damages the health of those around you
- Stopping smoking reduces the risk of serious disease
- Smoking causes cancer, chronic bronchitis and other chest diseases
- More than (...) people die each year in (name of country) from lung cancer
- Every year, (...) people are killed in road accidents in (name of country) – (...) times more die from their addiction to smoking
- Every year, addiction to smoking claims more victims than road accidents
- Smokers die younger
- Don't smoke if you want to stay healthy
- Save money: stop smoking

Health warnings
These are four of the images printed on cigarette packets in Canada to warn people about the results of smoking.

Plans are in place in the EU to limit the tar, nicotine and carbon monoxide content of a cigarette to 10 mg tar, 1 mg nicotine and 10 mg carbon monoxide. It is also proposed that these regulations should apply to cigarettes made for export as well as those sold within the EU.

The strongest messages are seen on cigarette packs sold in Canada. Since December 2000, cigarette manufacturers have had to print one of 16 new health warnings. Each of these is accompanied by a graphic image, for example, 'Cigarettes cause mouth diseases' followed by 'Cigarette smoke causes oral cancer, gum diseases and tooth loss' with a photo of a smoker's open mouth and teeth.

Lawsuits

In recent years there have been a number of court cases, particularly in the USA, where smokers with lung cancer and other smoking-related diseases have sued the tobacco companies for damages. As the number of people suffering from these diseases increases, so do the medical costs to health services. In November 1998, the tobacco industry agreed to pay 50 states in the USA a total of $246 billion over a number of years. This is to compensate for the billions of taxpayers' dollars spent on treating smoking-related illnesses. Now the states are deciding how to spend this money.

A case lost

Norwegian Robert Lund (right) shakes hands with the head of Tiedemanns tobacco company before a newsworthy court case in 2000. Lund had lung cancer and sued the company for not warning him of the dangers of smoking and for causing his illness. Lund (a smoker since the 1950s) died before the end of the case. The court ruled against him, saying that tobacco's addictiveness did not free him from responsibility: he had continued to smoke even after the dangers had become widely known and accepted. His family said they would appeal.

Class actions

In July 2000, a court case in Florida made legal history. A jury ordered five of the world's largest tobacco companies to pay an unprecedented $145 billion in damages for harming thousands of smokers living in Florida. This was also the first successful 'class action', in which the case was fought on behalf of thousands of unidentified people, rather than named individuals. As expected, the case has now gone to appeal, and it is likely that the ruling will be overturned. If it is not, each of the 700,000 smokers in Florida would have to go to court to make their own claim for a share of the damages, so the case could go on for decades. Class actions in 28 other states have failed, mainly because smoking was considered to be the responsibility of the individual.

4 Passive smoking
Cigarettes and non-smokers

No choice
A child in Bangladesh suffers from his carer's smoking.

Passive smoking is the inhaling of other people's smoke. A non-smoker sitting beside a smoker breathes in both the side-stream smoke from the burning tip of the cigarette and the main-stream smoke that has been inhaled and then exhaled by the smoker. In fact, the smoke released from the lit end of a cigarette often contains greater amounts of nicotine and carbon monoxide than the smoke that is inhaled by the smoker, since it has not passed through a filter. Not surprisingly, non-smokers are concerned that breathing in other people's smoke could be harmful to their health.

Health risks

Some of the immediate effects of passive smoking include eye irritation, headache, cough, sore throat, dizziness and nausea. Anyone who suffers from asthma can experience a significant reduction in their lung function when they are exposed to smoke, and new cases of asthma may be induced in children whose parents smoke.

In the longer term, passive smokers suffer an increased risk of a range of smoking-related diseases. Smoking causes most cases of lung cancer, but a small percentage have been linked to passive smoking. For example, non-smokers who are exposed to passive smoking in the home have as much as a 25 per cent increased risk of heart disease and lung cancer. About 600 non-smokers die from lung cancer each year in the UK and about 3,000 in the USA. One of the best-known cases involved an entertainer, Roy Castle, a lifelong non-smoker who died from lung cancer. He attributed his cancer to years of working in clubs where smoking was permitted.

Entertainment
Roy Castle blamed his lung cancer on the smoky atmosphere of jazz clubs, where he used to play. Before he died, he worked hard to publicize the dangers of smoking.

The US Environmental Protection Agency has been studying the risks of passive smoking compared with other carcinogens in the environment. It found that the lifelong risk from passive smoking was more than 100 times higher than the estimated effect of 20 years of exposure to asbestos, a carcinogen found in old buildings.

There have been numerous studies into the link between passive smoking and lung cancer, but the number of cases involved was fairly low. In 1998, the widely differing results of two large studies were published. The WHO's International Agency for Research on Cancer (IARC) found little or no increased risk of lung cancer from exposure to tobacco smoke in the home, at work, in vehicles or in indoor public settings, such as restaurants. In contrast, the SCOTH report (Report of the Scientific Committee on Tobacco and Health, UK) concluded that for people with long-term exposure to environmental tobacco smoke the increased risk of lung cancer was about 20-30 per cent.

Asthma
A child living with smokers is twice as likely to develop asthma.

Smoking in the home

Despite the arguments about the link between smoking and lung cancer, most doctors agree that environmental tobacco smoke has harmful effects on children. Children living with parents who smoke have been found to be less healthy than children living in smoke-free homes.

Children who live in smoking households are more likely to suffer from a number of respiratory diseases, such as bronchitis and pneumonia. A study in 1999 by the International Consultation on Environmental Tobacco Smoke and Child Health found that in households where both parents smoke, young children have a 72 per cent increased risk of respiratory illnesses. Children in smoking homes have twice the risk of developing asthma and they suffer from more coughs and colds. These children also receive an amount of nicotine equivalent to smoking 80 cigarettes per year.

The risks of parental smoking on children include:

- Sudden Infant Death Syndrome or cot death (25 per cent linked to smoking)
- 30 per cent greater likelihood of developing middle ear disease or glue ear, the commonest cause of deafness in children

- increased incidence of asthma
- poor lung function
- more coughs and colds
- greater likelihood of being admitted to hospital for bronchitis and pneumonia in the first year of life
- development of respiratory disease in adult life

'I didn't think the odd cigarette would hurt my baby. But when I went for an antenatal check-up the nurse told me about the dangers of smoking while pregnant. I stopped straight away.' (Gloria)

Harm to the unborn child

The presence of nicotine, carbon monoxide and tar in the body of a pregnant woman can damage the development of her unborn child. Smoking during pregnancy results in babies with a lower than average birth weight. Babies who were exposed before birth to their mother's cigarette smoke have been found to grow up with reduced lung function and an air flow to their lungs that is up to 6 per cent below normal. Studies in California showed that children born to women who smoked 10 or more cigarettes a day after the fourth month of pregnancy made poorer progress at school up to the age of 16.

Despite the health warnings displayed in antenatal clinics, many women still smoke during their pregnancy. In the UK, 23 per cent of women smokers smoke throughout pregnancy, and a further 33 per cent smoke at some point during their pregnancy. And the men are no better! Only a small number of men give up smoking when their partners become pregnant.

In pregnant women, smoking leads to an increased risk of:

- spontaneous abortion (miscarriage)
- bleeding during pregnancy
- premature birth
- low weight of babies at birth (which is associated with greater risks of ill-health and failure to thrive)
- Sudden Infant Death Syndrome (cot death).

No smoking areas

Increasingly, public buildings, offices, schools, hospitals and transport systems in Europe, North America, parts of Southeast Asia and Australasia are becoming no-smoking zones. In Singapore and parts of California, it is illegal to smoke anywhere in public, including out of doors. These controls are to protect the non-smoking public from the harmful effects of passive smoking. In contrast, there are few, if any controls, in Eastern Europe, many Asian and African countries, and Central and South America.

Banned
Smokers gather outside their non-smoking work-place.

Some of these controls are through government legislation. For example, in 1988, the UK's Independent Scientific Committee on Smoking and Health recommended that non-smoking should be regarded as the norm in enclosed areas used by the public or employees and special provision should be made for smokers, rather than vice versa.

No smoking
In Taiwan, smoking has been banned since 1997 in all public areas, including aeroplanes and hotels.

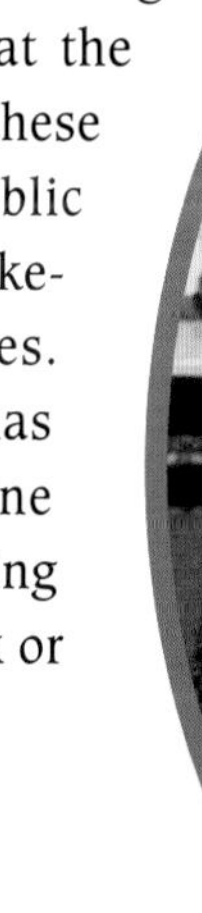

Consumer pressure is forcing rapid change in restaurants, cinemas and leisure facilities. Studies of the economic impact of introducing no-smoking areas in restaurants show that the majority of customers think these are a good idea. Most public transport systems are smoke-free, as are many planes. Pressure from non-smokers has persuaded many airline companies to offer no-smoking flights, even on journeys of six or more hours.

A smoke-free office

I don't smoke, so I really objected to people in my office lighting up at their desks. Despite air conditioning, the air was still smoky. I had to breathe their smoke whether I liked it or not. I went home each night with a headache and smoky clothes that had to go straight in the wash. The smoke was affecting my health. A chain smoker joined the team and things got so bad that the non-smokers made an official complaint to the management. Now the office has been made 'no smoking' throughout and the smokers have to leave the building if they want a cigarette.
(Liam, accounts manager)

5 Kicking the habit
How to stop smoking and stay stopped

Many adult smokers say that they know about the risks of smoking – the effect on their health, the smells, the cost, even the inconvenience of having to smoke outside the back door at home or at work. They don't want to give up because they are addicted to nicotine. Beating the addiction is the key to giving up smoking successfully.

Giving up
It is easier to give up smoking completely than to try to reduce your smoking gradually.

Persuading young smokers to give up is even more difficult. One of the problems with smoking is that the effects are long-term. The damage builds up over a number of years. There are a few early-warning signs, such as the early-morning cough and shortness of breath, but these are often ignored, or considered to be one of the downsides of smoking. Today, many young people are unfit as a result of their sedentary lifestyles – sitting in front of the TV or computer and being driven in the car – so perhaps they don't notice that their lung capacity is a fraction of what it should be. A long and painful death from lung cancer seems remote to a 15 year-old. So it's not surprising that smoking has been likened to slow-motion suicide.

There are various ways of kicking the smoking habit. Whichever way is chosen, the effect on health is almost immediate. Within days, the ex-smoker will have fewer coughs, cleaner clothes and easier breathing. Lung capacity improves and the ex-smoker will soon feel fitter. The risk of heart disease decreases too, especially during the first year.

One of the most difficult aspects of giving up smoking is beating the nicotine addiction. Giving up this drug is difficult and the person will suffer from withdrawal symptoms, such as irritability and restlessness. Fortunately, these effects disappear after a few weeks.

Help yourself to quit

People may tell you that it is easier to cut down on the number of cigarettes you smoke each day than to make a clean break. Although this might seem a good idea, it is difficult to do in practice. If you cut down, the likely response is that you will smoke each cigarette more intensively and end up doing yourself as much harm as before. Smoking just a few cigarettes brings you into contact with the nicotine, and every few days you have to go into a shop to buy a fresh supply. This makes it even more difficult to stop smoking completely.

There are four phases to giving up cigarettes:

- thinking about stopping
- preparing to stop
- stopping
- staying stopped.

Reasons to stop

Here are just a few reasons why you might want to stop:

- *lower risk of cancer*
- *lower risk of heart attacks*
- *living a longer and healthier life*
- *having more money to spend on other things*
- *a better chance of having a healthy baby*
- *food and drink taste better*
- *a better skin and complexion and fewer wrinkles*
- *fresher-smelling breath, hair and clothes*
- *easier to travel on trains, planes and buses*
- *concern about environmental impact of tobacco growing.*

Thinking about stopping

One of the keys to success is really wanting to stop, and willpower has a tremendous role to play. So before you stop, think about the benefits of stopping – a healthier body and a longer life, fresher breath and smoke-free clothes. Work out how much money you will save and plan how to spend it.

'I'm going to stop smoking on my birthday. That's in two weeks time. My girlfriend is determined to make sure I stop. She's arranged for me to go to the match with a few mates and then we're going out for dinner followed by a late film, so she can keep a close eye on me!'
(James, 19)

Stay busy
Make sure you keep busy all day so you have no time to think about that cigarette!

Preparing to stop

For many people, smoking is a habit that is linked to certain times of day, places and friends. It's important to break as many of these links as possible. So before you actually stop, think about when and where you smoke. These times and places are danger spots. Work out in advance how to avoid situations where you instinctively want a cigarette, and how to avoid the company of other smokers and places where you will be tempted to smoke or can buy cigarettes. Sometimes it helps to occupy your day with a new activity. This will prevent you thinking about smoking. Try to get help from family and friends. Tell them you are stopping so that they can offer support and encouragement. Make sure you can call a friend if you feel like smoking so he or she can talk you through it. Stressful times, when you would have naturally smoked a cigarette, will be the worst.

Stopping

Choose a day to stop completely. Make sure the chosen day will not be too stressful. Then get rid of all your cigarettes, ashtrays and lighters. The first day will be important. Make sure you have plenty to do. You could get up late and have a long relaxing bath, go for a long walk or play some sport. And it's just as important to plan a treat for yourself at the end of the day. Don't sit around thinking about smoking – keep busy and distract yourself. Keep reminding yourself that just because you want a cigarette it doesn't mean you have to have one.

It's now that the first signs of nicotine withdrawal will make themselves felt. You may feel restless, irritable, unable to concentrate, unable to sleep and accident-prone. You may experience mood swings, feeling happy one minute and depressed the next. But don't give in – these things will pass and you will quickly start to feel the benefits.

Yoga
Some people find yoga a good way to help them relax.

Staying stopped

Take it a day at a time. Each day try to stop for one more day. Think positively. If you are offered a cigarette say 'No thanks, I don't smoke'. Give yourself lots to do – tidy your bedroom, do the washing, go to places where smoking is not allowed, take up a new sport or start jogging. During the first week, you will start to feel the benefits of not smoking but you may experience a bad cough. This is the first phase of cleaning out your lungs. You may miss the calming effects of a cigarette, so learn to relax. You can learn techniques that help you to relax naturally, such as meditation and yoga.

'I have often been tempted to start again. It has been hard. I still tell myself that staying off the cigs is like a game of snakes and ladders. Just one drag on a cigarette would send me down the longest snake right back to square one. And there's no way I want to go back and do it all again.'
(Maxine, ex-smoker)

Don't let yourself be fooled into thinking one cigarette won't hurt – it will. After one, you'll want another and another. A clean break is best. Keep reminding yourself of all the health benefits and the fact that you won't want to go through 'giving up' again.

Giving up

The first day was just terrible and it seemed as if it lasted forever. I had picked a Saturday as my stop-smoking day. I got up and the very first thing I thought about was a cigarette. It's not normally like that but maybe because I knew I couldn't have a cigarette I couldn't get it out of my mind. I went shopping with a friend. It's amazing just how many shops sell cigarettes – they kept jumping out at me. Every time I stopped to look, my friend would drag me past. I didn't feel great and was I in a bad mood! I snapped at everybody. I was supposed to go out with friends for the evening but I couldn't face being nice to them so I stayed in. I tried watching television. I wandered round the flat, tried reading some magazines, but I couldn't concentrate. Then I listened to a couple of CDs. Great – it was time for bed but I couldn't get to sleep. As I lay in bed all I could think of was cigarettes. Finally I fell asleep but I didn't feel much better when I woke up. Day two was just as bad. So was day three, but at least I was in college for the day and had lectures to go to. I don't know exactly when I stopped thinking about cigarettes. I suddenly realized that I hadn't thought about a cigarette all afternoon. The first week was the worst. After about four days I started to cough – that was disgusting. Far worse than any morning cough I had had before. By the next weekend things were better. I went to see a movie with some friends, which was good because the cinema was non-smoking. Looking back I can't believe I stuck it out. But I did and I definitely don't want to go through that again – ever.
(Sandra, ex-smoker)

Giving up smoking can be tough and requires lots of willpower. Most people find the first few days difficult and for some it can be a long struggle, but things will usually start to get better after the third or fourth day. Many people will not succeed the first time. Don't worry. You can always try again.

Nicotine replacement therapies

If willpower alone does not work and you can't beat the addiction, you can use nicotine chewing gum, lozenges, inhalers or nicotine patches to help stop the craving for the drug. The chances of successfully giving up smoking are doubled by using nicotine replacement therapies. These allow the ex-smoker to come off nicotine gradually by using a low dose of the drug to take the edge off the craving and give a 'soft landing'. The transdermal nicotine patch is like a sticky plaster and is worn on the upper arm during the day. It releases a steady stream of nicotine into the blood. The nicotine inhaler is a hand-held device designed to overcome the physical craving for nicotine and the behavioural dependence of handling cigarettes. Some lozenges, capsules and tablets contain small doses of nicotine and aim to reduce the craving; others contain silver acetate, which produces an unpleasant taste when a cigarette is smoked. Unfortunately, few of these products have been clinically tested, but they have been found to help many people.

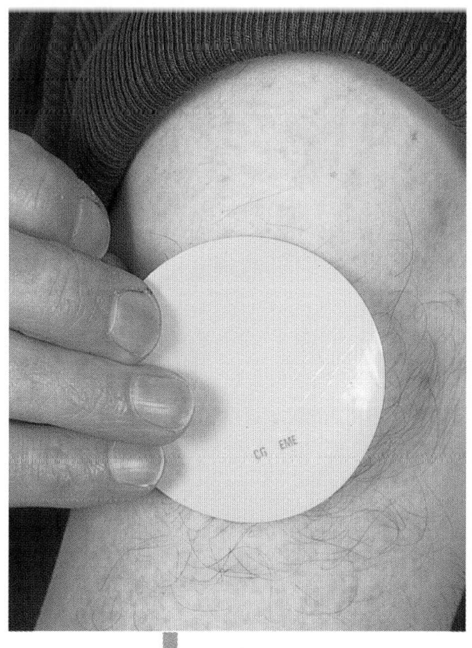

Patch
A nicotine patch slowly releases nicotine through the skin and into the bloodstream.

Zyban

In 1997 a new anti-smoking treatment became available. It is a little-known anti-depressant called bupropion, with the trade name Zyban – a drug that reduces the craving for nicotine. It is the first quitting aid that is not based on substituting nicotine in tobacco with another form of nicotine. Zyban is available only on prescription. First the patient takes the drug twice daily for two weeks while they are still smoking. Then they stop smoking but continue to take the drug for a further 12 weeks.

'I've been a smoker for 36 years and have been through things you wouldn't believe, trying to stop. But Zyban seems to be a miracle! I can handle cravings – they're more like thoughts about a cigarette, really. Real cravings have been few.' (Gail)

Zyban is an anti-depressant that works directly in the brain. It disrupts the addictive nature of nicotine by affecting the same chemical messengers. One of the pleasurable effects of nicotine is its release of dopamine from brain cells. Smoking floods the brain with dopamine. Zyban causes the release of dopamine, but in much smaller quantities. This treatment seems to be more successful than the nicotine replacement therapies but as always there is an element of willpower involved. Zyban can also be used with nicotine-replacement aids to increase further the chances of quitting.

Getting help

If you find you still can't stop, there are many professional and self-help groups that can offer help and support. Your doctor, pharmacist or health visitor should be able to give advice and tell you if there are special services for smokers in your area. Some people try hypnosis, acupuncture, aversion therapy and relaxation classes. There is little evidence to support the effectiveness of either acupuncture or hypnosis as a means of stopping smoking, but some smokers have found such methods to be useful.

Herbal cigarettes

Some people turn to herbal cigarettes, but these can cause just as many problems as tobacco. Herbal cigarettes produce tar and carbon monoxide, and some brands have a tar content equivalent to tobacco cigarettes. Furthermore, the use of herbal cigarettes reinforces the habit of smoking which smokers need to overcome.

Weight watching

Many people, especially women, worry about putting on weight when they stop smoking. Nicotine changes the appetite and increases the body's metabolism, so that it burns up more energy. As a result, four in every five smokers gain weight when they stop smoking. The average weight gain is about 3 kg, but this can be lost in a couple of weeks once the person has finally stopped smoking, for example, by changing the diet, avoiding alcohol and taking more exercise. The rapid improvement in lung function will make exercise that much easier.

National campaigns

Many governments and organizations, such as the WHO, sponsor campaigns to persuade people to stop smoking. These may take the form of adverts on TV and in national newspapers and campaigns in schools. There have even been TV programmes to help people give up, with ordinary people appearing on them each week. These programmes form a type of national support group, and there are books, leaflets and websites to accompany them.

Examples

A billboard in Times Square, New York, shows non-smoking sports and entertainment personalities.

In the UK, there is an annual No Smoking Day. In the USA, the America Cancer Society organizes the 'Great American Smoke-out', which aims to get as many of the 48 million smokers as possible to stop for the day. There is also a 'Kick Butts Day' on 4 April which is aimed at stopping children from smoking. The WHO organizes the World No Tobacco Day on 31 May. Many people find a no-smoking day to be a good one for stopping smoking as they will not be alone in trying to give up on that day.

Beneficial health changes when you stop smoking

TIME SINCE QUITTING	*BENEFICIAL HEALTH CHANGES*
20 minutes	*Blood pressure and pulse rate return to normal.*
8 hours	*Nicotine and carbon monoxide levels in blood fall by 50 per cent and oxygen levels return to normal.*
24 hours	*No more carbon monoxide in the body. Lungs start to clear out mucus and other smoking debris.*
48 hours	*No nicotine left in the body. Senses of taste and smell are greatly improved.*
72 hours	*Breathing becomes easier and energy levels increase.*
2-12 weeks	*Circulation improves.*
3-9 months	*Fewer coughs, wheezes and breathing problems. Lung function is increased by up to 10 per cent.*
5 years	*Risk of a heart attack falls to about half that of a smoker.*
10 years	*Risk of lung cancer falls to half that of a smoker. Risk of heart attack falls to the same as someone who has never smoked.*

'It's easier not to start than it is to stop'

Christy Turlington, a well-known model, was a heavy smoker for many years before she finally managed to quit. In 1997, her father died of lung cancer. Since then she has become actively involved in a campaign to educate teenagers about addiction to tobacco products. In a 30 second television commercial in which she tells viewers how she quit smoking and lost her father to lung cancer, Christy says:

'In my life, there are two people in my family who have quit smoking. Me and my Dad. For me it took seven years. Nothing worked. When I finally did quit for good, I knew it was one of the biggest accomplishments of my life. My Dad, it was different for him. He stopped December 1996, just six months before he died from lung cancer.'

Resources

Books

Rob Alcraft, *Need to Know: Tobacco*, Heinemann Library, 2000
A factual book about tobacco, aimed at teenagers. It includes a range of real-life case studies and experiences and detailed information on the effects of smoking on the individual and society.

Martin Raw, *Kick the Habit. How to Stop Smoking and Stay Stopped*, BBC Consumer Publishing, 2000
This book outlines how to plan to stop smoking. It explains why it is hard to stop and describes the importance of motivation and preparation. It guides the smoker through the process of stopping.

Gillian Riley, *How to Stop and Stay Stopped for Good*, Vermilion, 1997
This book aims to teach the smoker how to control the desire for a cigarette without gaining weight or feeling irritable, depressed or deprived.

Angela Royston, *Learn to Say No: Smoking*, Heinemann Library, 2000
An introduction to the facts about smoking, its history and the physical and social effects of smoking. The book aims to teach young people not to smoke and provides lots of strategies to help them avoid becoming involved in smoking.

Videos

Seven ages of Moron
A black comedy featuring Mel Smith and Griff Rhys-Jones, published by the Cancer Research Campaign. (This video was produced about 12 years ago but is still informative and entertaining.)

SLAM
A 15-minute video produced by The Center for Disease Control and Prevention's Office on Smoking and Health. It tells the story of Leslie Nuchow, a talented but unsigned young singer-songwriter, who refused to have her music associated with a cigarette marketing campaign targeted at young people. The video helps young people be more aware of the power and persuasiveness of cigarette advertising and to explore ways to resist the influences of the tobacco industry.

Websites

Action on Smoking and Health
www.ash.org.uk
Provides lots of factual information about smoking, ways of stopping smoking, press releases and links to other sites.

British American Tobacco
www.bat.com
Find out what the tobacco industry has to say. This site provides information about British American Tobacco – what it is, what it does, what it believes – and includes press releases, etc.

Campaign for Tobacco-free Kids
tobaccofreekids.org (Note: no www)
A site aimed at teenagers, with plenty of information and fact sheets.

Cancerhelp
www.cancerhelp.org.uk
This site is run by the Cancer Research Council and provides plenty of information on cancers: the different types, symptoms, diagnosis, treatments and help groups. There is a large section on lung cancer.

National Centre for Chronic Disease Prevention and Health Promotion
www.cdc.gov/tobacco
Provides data, tables, results of smoking surveys and plenty of educational material.

National Smokers Alliance
www.speak-up.org
A site for smokers. This large campaigning organization wants the freedom to make personal choices.

Quitsmoking
www.quitsmoking.about.com/health/quitsmoking/mbody.htm
Provides lots of information about giving up smoking as well as chat rooms and discussion groups. There are links to many other smoking-related sites.

World Health Organization, Tobacco Free Initiative
tobacco.who.int (Note: no www)
Comprehensive site giving details of worldwide anti-smoking campaigns, such as World No Tobacco Day and data on smoking in Europe.

Sources used for this book

C. Blair, *Predicting the onset of smoking in boys and girls*, Social Science and Medicine, 1989
J. Wilkinson, *Tobacco: The facts behind the smokescreen*, Penguin, 1986

Action on Smoking and Health (ASH), various articles and leaflets
National Centre for Chronic Disease Prevention and Health Promotion, website
British American Tobacco, website and promotional materials
World Health Organization, *Smoke Free Europe*, 1989

Smoking and Pollution, materials published by the Health Education Authority Family Smoking Project
Articles in the *British Medical Journal*, *Health Education Journal*, *New Scientist*

Glossary

addiction a condition in which a person takes a drug regularly and cannot stop taking it without experiencing symptoms of withdrawal.

alveoli (singular alveolus) tiny air-filled sacs in the lungs, with walls one cell thick and surrounded by capillaries. They provide a large surface area over which oxygen and carbon dioxide can be exchanged between air and blood.

bronchitis an inflammation of the bronchi and bronchioles, leading to difficulty in breathing.

cancer a malignant growth or tumour produced by the uncontrolled division of cells.

carbon monoxide a colourless, odourless gas released when carbon-containing substances are burnt, for example, tobacco and fossil fuels.

carcinogen a chemical that has been found to cause cancer.

cardiovascular relating to the heart and circulation.

chemotherapy the treating of cancerous growths or tumours using powerful drugs that seek out and kill cancerous cells.

dependence a condition in which the body relies on the presence of a substance.

dopamine a chemical released by nerve cells in the brain. It affects the brain processes that control movement, emotional responses and the ability to experience pain and pleasure.

hormone a chemical messenger, produced by endocrine or ductless glands in the body, which affects other parts of the body. For example, the hormone adrenalin is produced by the adrenal gland and affects the heart.

menopause the time during which a woman's periods gradually stop. It is a time of great hormonal change and adjustment.

menstruation the monthly discharge of blood from the lining of the uterus in women. Each cycle lasts about 28 days.

nicotine a poisonous chemical found in tobacco, with addictive properties. It can be lethal if injected into the body, but it is not lethal when inhaled.

oncogene a gene that can change a normal cell into a cancerous one.

passive smoking the inhalation of cigarette smoke by a non-smoker, which can affect his or her health.

peer-group pressure the influence of an individual or individuals on the behaviour of people of the same age or interests.

side-stream smoke smoke released from the lit end of a cigarette that is not inhaled by the smoker.

withdrawal the process of ceasing to take an addictive drug, which may be accompanied by unpleasant side effects.

Index